Conference Report

The Political Stability

of Italy

The Center for Strategic
and International Studies
Georgetown University
April 2, 1976

Contents

Preface

This conference, held April 2, 1976, was designed to explore recent political, economic, and social trends in Italy, one of the closest and most important allies of the United States. Italy is always a factor in international power equations because it sits astride the strategic crossroads of the Mediterranean Sea and constitutes a vital element in the southern flank of the North Atlantic Treaty Organization.

Today a portentious political debate is raging both in Italy and elsewhere in Europe over the possible entry of the Communist Party of Italy into the Italian Government, and its effects on the future security of the Mediterranean region and all of West Europe.

Some experts see the concept of a revolutionary "Historic Compromise" between the Italian Communists and the center political parties as a new face for West European Communism, distancing Communist parties in the West from Moscow. Others see it as a tactical maneuver bound to end in weakening democratic government in Italy. Still others see it as a betrayal of the political left. Whatever the current political ferment brings, it is bound to affect the foreign policy and strategic interests of the United States in crucial ways. The discussions at this conference were intended to call attention to and shed light on these political problems.

Ray S. Cline
Director of Studies, CSIS

Program

The Political Stability
of Italy: Afternoon Session

OPENING REMARKS: Dr. Ray S. Cline
Conference Chairman and
Director of Studies, CSIS

PANEL DISCUSSION: **THE POLITICAL PROBLEMS OF ITALY IN THE
EUROPEAN-MEDITERRANEAN CONTEXT**

    Panel Chairman: The Honorable John B. Connally
Former Secretary of the Treasury

    Panelists: The Honorable William E. Colby
Former Director,
Central Intelligence Agency

Admiral Horacio Rivero, USN (Ret.)
Former U.S. Ambassador to Spain

Ms. Claire Sterling
Freelance Journalist, Rome, Italy

Program

The Political Stability of Italy: Evening Session

DINNER DISCUSSION: **SUMMARY OF HIGHLIGHTS OF PANEL DISCUSSION**

The Honorable John B. Connally
Panel Chairman

ADDRESS: "U.S. Foreign Policy and Italy"
The Honorable Clare Boothe Luce
Former U.S. Ambassador to Italy

Biography

John B. Connally

The Honorable John B. Connally was born in Texas and received his law degree from the University of Texas in 1941. In 1949 he was administrative assistant to then Senator Lyndon B. Johnson. Besides being a senior partner of a prestigious law firm based in Houston, he has served his state and his nation with distinction, first as Secretary of the Navy, then as Governor of Texas, and then as Secretary of the Treasury. He is a member of the President's Foreign Intelligence Advisory Board and his counsel has been sought by four of America's presidents.

Now, as a private citizen, he continues to speak out in many public forums on issues he considers vital to our nation's future.

Biography

William E. Colby

The Honorable William E. Colby was born in St. Paul, Minnesota, graduated from Princeton University in 1940, and joined the United States Army in 1941. Later during the war he parachuted behind enemy lines in central France, then in northern Norway for the Office of Strategic Services (OSS). Mr. Colby received distinguished service awards not only from the U.S., but also from France, Norway, and Great Britain.

Following the war, Mr. Colby obtained his law degree from Columbia Law School and worked a couple of years for the New York law firm headed by William J. "Wild Bill" Donovan, former head of OSS. He is a member of the New York State and U.S. Supreme Court bars. Mr. Colby then returned to government service and served abroad in the American Embassies in Stockholm, in Rome, and in Saigon. During 1968–1971 he served in Vietnam as Assistant Chief of Staff and later Deputy to the Commander of the U.S. Military Assistance Command (MACV), in charge of support to the Government of Vietnam's pacification program. He held the personal rank of Ambassador.

In 1973 Mr. Colby was appointed as Director of the Central Intelligence Agency and served in that capacity until very recently.

Biography

Clare Boothe Luce

The Honorable Clare Boothe Luce was born—simply as Clare Boothe—and educated in New York City. Because of her outstanding achievements in a many-faceted career, she has received honors, awards, and honorary degrees from many institutions, including degrees from Fordham University, Temple University, Mt. Holyoke College, and Georgetown University.

Mrs. Luce began her career as an Associate Editor of *Vogue Magazine* and continued later as Managing Editor of *Vanity Fair*. She was—and still is—a successful newspaper columnist, has written three books and seven plays, including the fantastically successful *The Women*, first produced in 1937.

From 1943–47 Mrs. Luce served as Member of Congress from Connecticut and from 1953–57 held the post of U.S. Ambassador to Italy.

Mrs Luce is currently a member of the President's Foreign Intelligence Advisory Board as well as a member of the National Commission on the Observance of International Women's Year (IWY).

She continues to write and speak on public issues, residing in Hawaii and, at intervals, in Washington, D.C.

Biography

Horacio Rivero, Jr.

Admiral Horacio Rivero was born in Ponce, Puerto Rico, in 1910, was graduated from the U.S. Naval Academy with distinction, third in his class, and commissioned in 1931.

Admiral Rivero has had lots of sea duty on board the battleships *New Mexico, California* and *Pennsylvania*, in cruisers and destroyers. He served in posts of increasingly high responsibility in the Navy Department in Washington, at Pacific Fleet Headquarters and Atlantic Fleet Headquarters.

In 1962 Admiral Rivero assumed command of the Atlantic Fleet Amphibious Force and received an award for his actions during the Cuban crisis of 1962. He became Vice Chief of Naval Operations in 1964 and served three and a half years in that position. From 1968 to 1972 Admiral Rivero was in command of Allied Forces Southern Europe, one of the three major military commands of Allied Command Europe. AFSOUTH is tasked with the defense of NATO's entire southern region—the countries of Greece, Italy and Turkey and the Mediterranean Sea.

Admiral Rivero is much decorated, his awards including the Bronze Star for his part in Guadalcanal, the Gilbert and Santa Cruz Islands, the Legion of Merit and the Distinguished Service Medal, both with gold stars.

Admiral Rivero's last public service post was in diplomacy. In 1972 he was appointed Ambassador to Spain, where he served until 1974.

Biography

Claire Sterling

Claire Sterling was born in New York City, has a Bachelor's Degree in Economics from Brooklyn College, a Master's Degree in Journalism from Columbia University, and has been abroad for many years as a Rome-based correspondent. She wrote for the *Reporter Magazine* from 1951–1968, covering Italy in particular but also about 50 other countries from time to time in East and West Europe, the Middle East, the Mediterranean region, and black Africa. Since then, she has been writing on environmental and political subjects, with heavy emphasis on Italy, for the *New Republic, The Washington Post*, the Paris *Herald Tribune*, mostly as an editorial page columnist, as well as for *Harper's*, the *Atlantic Monthly*, *Reader's Digest*, and *The New York Times Sunday Magazine*. In 1970 she wrote a book about Czechoslovakia, called *The Masaryk Case* (published by Harper & Row). Her recent articles on current Italian political trends are some of the most informative pieces the American press has carried on the subject of this conference.

Biography

Ray S. Cline

Ray S. Cline, who holds a Ph.D. from Harvard University and was Prize Fellow at Balliol College, Oxford, joined the Georgetown University Center for Strategic and International Studies (CSIS) in 1973 as Executive Director of Studies in charge of all CSIS internal research. He formerly served more than 30 years as a government official, in later years in such senior positions as Deputy Director for Intelligence of the Central Intelligence Agency (1962–1966) and Director of Intelligence and Research in the Department of State (1969–1973). He was awarded a Distinguished Intelligence Service Medal and a Career Intelligence Medal.

Dr. Cline is author of the following publications:

Washington Command Post, 1951, an analysis of U.S. military planning in World War II;

"Policy Without Intelligence," *Foreign Policy,* Winter 1974-1975 issue, Number 17, an article suggesting better use of intelligence as it relates to collecting hard-to-get information abroad, analyzing it in a foreign policy context, and reporting it at the National Security Council level;

World Power Assessment: A Calculus of Strategic Drift, (Georgetown University-CSIS) 1975, an evaluation of trends in international power politics.

xxi

Conference Report

Afternoon Session

Conference Chairman Dr. Ray S. Cline, Executive Director of Studies at CSIS, opened the meeting by stating that the conference should examine "trends affecting the political stability of one of the great Western industrial democracies: Italy." He said:

"Surely it is our responsibility in the United States to ponder thoughtfully the strategic issues at stake in present-day Italian political trends of an unprecedented character. We must see our strategic interests clearly if we are to exercise our great power wisely . . . . I can think of no theme that has emerged in recent months with greater clarity and urgency than this one: what are the prospects for political stability in Italy, and what does this mean for the European and Mediterranean world in which the United States has crucial strategic interests at stake?"

Connally Sounds Alarm

Former Treasury Secretary John B. Connally, chairman of the panel, said that the region to be discussed "was the cradle of civilization. It is not beyond reason that it could also become its grave."

Mr. Connally was openly critical of the policy of détente. "It is my belief," he said, "that we have entered an extremely dangerous period of history, comparable, in fact, to the decade prior to the Second World War. It disturbs me, frankly, that many Americans are unwilling to accept the warning signs . . . . Perhaps we are so anxious to reject the cold war mentality of a few years ago that we are blind to the expansionist policies of the Soviet Union."

The world, Mr. Connally continued, has moved "quietly and almost unnoticed into a new and perilous era—conceivably an era of reckoning for Western civilization and freedom."

This is an era of remarkable Soviet successes, he declared, and despite Moscow's conflict with China and the pullback from Egypt, "this has been a rewarding decade for Soviet expansionism."

Americans, Mr. Connally went on, are "too quick to draw back from the dangers that threaten us over the rim of the world. I am concerned that we doubt our capacity to lead." He urged Americans to renew their responsibilities for "economic and military leadership in a divided world" because that may "determine whether truly there will be peace in our time or the terrible alternative."

Speaking about the topic before the conference, he said it seems that "all of the problems of the world suddenly have descended on the countries of the Mediterranean." He listed these problems as the crisis in Lebanon, the Israeli-Arab question, the issue of Cyprus, the uncertain fate of Yugoslavia after Tito, the tension between Algeria and Morocco, the political turmoil in post-Franco Spain, the political and economic problems of Portugal, the possibility of a Socialist-Communist coalition government in France, and the prospect of a Communist takeover in Italy "with dire consequences for the Western Alliance."

"How long will the 'benevolent' and 'efficient' Communist Party of Italy be concerned with freedom of speech, freedom of the press, and tolerance of other political parties?" Mr. Connally asked. "No other Communist regime in history has demonstrated such liberal tendencies for very long—only long enough to suit its purposes," he declared.

In conclusion he said:

"Someday, somehow, the United States must stop misleading its adversaries by inconsistent and uncertain words and deeds. It must make itself plain . . . . It must show maturity in world affairs. It must be alert, vital, open-handed and even-handed, and loyal to the cause it espouses, in times of darkness as well as sunshine."

Colby: The Historical Perspective

Former CIA Director William Colby said the conference should examine the question of whether one should believe the present leaders of the Italian Communists who pledge that they will observe the rules of democracy if they are accepted as a partner in the government.

"Political systems and political movements cannot be judged on the good faith of the individuals who happen to be in power, because they are, of course, changeable," Mr. Colby warned.

He recalled in detail the history of the Italian Communist Party since its establishment in 1921, how it followed faithfully the Moscow line when it was forced underground during the Fascist era, and how it became the leader of resistance against the Mussolini regime during World War II, "thanks to its experience in clandestine work and thanks to its hardening in the Spanish civil war."

Immediately after the Second World War the Italian Communists focused on creating what Colby called a mass base for their party, avoiding "the narrow belief that the Communists could do everything themselves." This did not go smoothly, the former intelligence chief said. The purists in the party, he explained, were distressed that their party had accepted a subordinate role in the post-war coalition government, and considered the concordat with the Vatican, concluded by this coalition government, "an extreme step."

The purists were also confused by what happened in Eastern Europe after the war, where the Red Army helped the Communist parties eliminate all opposition and create a one-party rule. But Stalin made it clear to the Communist parties of Western Europe that they could not count on him: "This was a clear reflection of his policy to give up an immediate bid for power in Western Europe as a price for developing a sphere of influence, indeed a security zone, in Eastern Europe," Colby said.

The Cold War marked the beginning of a difficult era for the Italian Communist Party, he went on. On orders from Moscow, the Italian Communists rejected the Marshall Plan with the consequence that the Socialists broke their alliance with the Communists, who were left "in single isolation."

But the coexistence policy of the 1960s, followed by détente, brought about another change. The Italian Communists, Colby said, "accepted coexistence, accepted the unity of Western Europe, and began to talk about the elimination of both NATO and the Warsaw Pact, perhaps thinking that the strengthening of European ties could bring about the weakening of Atlanticism, meaning the weakening of ties with the United States."

The 1968 Soviet aggression against Czechoslovakia provided the Italian Communists with the first real opportunity to prove that there was, as they claimed, an "Italian way to Communism.

"The party took a strong position challenging the validity of the Brezhnev doctrine . . . . They were talking about polycentrism," Colby said.

In the 1970s the Communists were encouraged by two things, Firstly, they interpreted the U.S. withdrawal from Vietnam and, later, U.S. hesitancy to intervene in Angola, as strong indications of neo-isolationism. Secondly, they witnessed "a decline in the power and effectiveness of the Vatican, when the Vatican took steps establishing diplomatic relations with Eastern European countries, replacing [Jozsef Cardinal] Mindszenty, signs indicating a desire to bridge the gap between Eastern Europe and Catholicism."

But, Colby said, the Italian Communists "have taken to heart" what happened in Chile and in Portugal. "They interpreted both events as indications that if they took steps that would lead too far, that would generate a reaction either from local forces or from the Americans."

It goes without saying, Colby declared, that the Italian Communist Party became "less doctrinaire in its approach toward ideological questions" than it used to be. The other side of the coin is, he warned, that the Italian Communists "still believe that they must maintain a link to the revolutionary center [i.e., Moscow] from which future support can be gained if things become difficult.

This does not mean that they are necessarily obedient to every order that comes from the center, but psychologically the Communist must feel that he is part of a world revolutionary movement."

Concluding, Colby said that "in relatively good times the Italian Communist Party has become more Italian, in relatively bad times it has become more Communist. The Party wants to be both . . . ."

Rivero: Effects on NATO

Admiral Horacio Rivero (USN, Ret.), former U.S. Ambassador to Spain, gave an alarming picture of the probable consequences of Communist domination of the Italian government from the military point of view.

"He who controls Italy controls the Mediterranean," the soldier-diplomat declared. Control of the Mediterranean, he explained, "means the ability to use the sea and the air above it in war. The bases in Italy and the Italian naval and air forces are needed for an effective defense of the Mediterranean against the surface and submarine threats that now exist."

The admiral said he was convinced that "accession to power of the Italian Communist Party, or a Communist-dominated government in Italy would result in an effective neutralization of that country." This, he continued, would carry with it "the eviction of NATO headquarters responsible for the defense of southern Europe, and of U.S. headquarters in charge of antisubmarine and submarine operations, the withdrawal of Italian forces from NATO and the elimination of the most important source of logistics, intelligence and communication support for the U.S. Sixth Fleet."

Under such circumstance, Admiral Rivero declared, "the early collapse of the entire southern flank would become inevitable and even the military balance in the central region of Europe would be adversely affected by the diversion to that front of strong Warsaw Pact forces now poised against Italy."

The further consequences would be, he went on, that the defense of Greece and Turkey would become increasingly difficult. These two allied countries can be effectively defended only by the "introduction of massive air power which can only come from the United States." With Italy neutralized, such air power could be rushed to the defense of Greece and Turkey only if Spain or France provided refueling facilities. But this, the admiral said, is a "very unlikely possibility. The Mediterranean is truly the lifeline of these two countries."

4

While U.S. naval forces based in Italy control the "choke point" between Italy and Tunisia, Italy's own naval and air forces complement the U.S. anti-submarine forces based in Sicily, the British forces in Malta, and the Sixth Fleet.

Even without a war situation, Admiral Rivero suggested, it was doubtful whether Turkey and Greece "could resist peacetime political pressures to seek accommodation with the Soviet Union on the latter's terms. The first Soviet demand would be to obtain some control over the Turkish straits."

The drastic shift in the military balance the admiral portrayed "could have decisive political effects also in the countries of North Africa and the Middle East." In addition, he said, "unilateral U.S. interests would be affected," as it would be extremely difficult for this country to provide effective assistance to Israel.

"Introduction of replacement war materiel to Israel would need to be done almost entirely by sea, unless air refueling of transport aircraft and of fighters could be carried out from Spain, a most unlikely prospect."

Should a Communist-dominated Italy follow the French and Greek examples by withdrawing from NATO's military structure but remaining in the Alliance, "the military effects would be essentially the same," Admiral Rivero continued. He said that while the theoretical possibility of such an Italy joining the Warsaw Pact cannot be ruled out, "to me this appears rather remote." But such an Italy, he suggested, may "follow the Yugoslav example." The picture would be even grimmer should the Soviets regain control over Yugoslavia after Tito. The effects on a Communist-dominated Italy would be "almost irresistible, the military difficulties for the United States and for NATO would be greatly magnified, and the Mediterranean would become a Soviet lake."

Eleanor Lansing Dulles, a retired diplomat, asked the admiral whether Germany could be used as a base should the use of the Italian bases be denied to the United States.

This would be almost impossible, Admiral Rivero replied. The West Germans would have to violate Swiss and/or Austrian neutrality. In addition, "the Germans would be busy in their own defense in the central front and could not divert forces to the southern flank."

Sterling Urges Realism

Ms. Claire Sterling, a journalist who has been living in Rome for 23 years, was the last panelist to speak.

She said at the outset that while she fully agreed with Admiral Rivero's military diagnosis, it would be a mistake to regard Italy as "simply a colored pin on the geopolitical map. Italy is a nation of 55 million people who are in extremely bad political, economic, and social trouble, seriously demoralized

5

and defeatist about the possibility of emerging from the crisis they are in, not only in the simplistic terms of whether the Communists will enter the government or not, but whether their state can survive."

Ms. Sterling was critical about "some of the words coming from Washington which sound unbelievably unreal." For the Italian, she said, the warning that Communist entrance into the Italian government is "unacceptable" has a hollow sound. "We may find it unacceptable but if we have no means of avoiding it, then what sense does it make to say so?" she asked.

It might be, she conceded, that such a "belligerent, militant, aggressive posture" may have some effect as many Italians continue to count on the United States to defend them from the Soviet Union. This, she added, is also true concerning some Italian Communists "who would like very much to be saved and protected from the Soviets." The other side of the coin is, however, that few Italians believe "the American public would tolerate open military intervention in Italy."

"The question whether the Communists do or do not enter the government is something only the Italians can decide," she declared.

Ms. Sterling acknowledged that the Italian Communists proved to be "enormously efficient politically" but added that "I do not know of any political party that has been helped so much by its enemies." She accused the "enemy", i.e., the Christian Democrats, of "total lack of conception of the meaning of the use of power" and blamed the United States for having allowed the Christian Democrats to believe that "whatever their failures, they will be always rescued.

"To this date there is no Italian who doubts that . . . the United States on its own, and by persuading Germany and by putting the heat on the members of the Common Market, would continue to bail out Italy year after year after year."

Even now, when the political crisis has reached its peak, the Christian Democrats "continue to think in terms of putting a patch of plaster over a spot of blood instead of thinking in terms of the total restructuring of the Italian economy," Ms. Sterling charged. The United States, she said, should have made it clear long ago that "simply because there always is the threat of Communism, the ruling political parties cannot get away with murder, with doing nothing except to enrich themselves and consolidate their own position.

"In that situation, frankly, I do not understand how we can say that it is unacceptable for the Communist Party to join the Italian Government, because there is no way in this world that we are going to stop it," she declared.

Communist Role in the Labor Crisis

The various Italian governments, Ms. Sterling went on, could remain in power only, "on sufferance of the Communists. . . . Government after government during the last 10–12 years has increasingly turned to the Communist Party for help to stay in power and this, in turn, has inevitably increased the strength of the Communist Party."

But the Communists can by no means dictate to Italy's industrial workers, especially not since 1969 when 12 million workers were on strike on and off between September and December. Since then it has become clear that "the Communists have been riding the tail, not leading the workers."

The wildcat strikes of 1969 hit first of all the government-controlled industries, which include more than half of the major industrial plants, Ms. Sterling explained. "These industries were in a state of panic and the government told its negotiators: 'go and settle for anything, give them everything, but settle.' And as soon the public sector was broken, the private sector had no capacity to resist."

This resulted in enormously increased labor costs, a "terribly disturbing feature" of the Italian economy since 1969, a primary factor in that country's economic crisis. There are others: the Statuti di Lavoratori, which permits "uncontrolled and unlimited absenteeism," and the Scala Mobile (sliding scale), which provides for an automatic increase of wages without collective bargaining.

The Communists, Ms. Sterling declared, did nothing to fight these two statutes which cripple the Italian economy. Moreover, when the new president of the Italian Central Bank suggested that the Scala Mobile should be suspended for six months, "the Communist Party flipped its lid, called it a shocking, unheard of proposal—and in fact it was never to be heard of again because no politician in Italy in his right mind would support such a proposal in times like this and in a country like Italy."

Personality vs. Doctrine

Ms. Sterling said she was "baffled" by statements made by a score of American intellectuals who seem to have become convinced that the Italian Communist Party "has indeed become a unique party which really means what it says, promising a most exciting new experiment which could revolutionize political history." These Americans were obviously charmed by the leaders of the Italian Communist Party who are "cultivated, charming, modern, extremely sophisticated, many of them contemptuous of the Soviet Union which, they believe, is a primitive model."

Based on her discussions with these leaders, she is convinced, Ms. Sterling said, that Carlo Payetta, whom she described as a "most professional Stalinist agit-prop man, would hate to live in an Italy converted after the Soviet model. Soviet dominance? Berlinguer would loathe it, Segre would find it intolerable," she said, referring to Enrico Berlinguer, head of the Italian Communist Party, and Sergio Segre, the "foreign minister" in the Communist shadow cabinet.

But there is no guarantee that these leaders will be around, or if they are, that they will not be forced to change their attitude once the Communists participate in the government, Ms. Sterling warned. Berlinguer, she said, is "a genuine gentleman, an intelligent man who really would like to give it a whirl, to try to create a sophisticated, industrialized, modern Communist state which would be as free as he could make it." But Berlinguer, "a reasonably honest man," conceded, when he was asked, that there was no guarantee that this attitude could be maintained should his party participate in power. Robespierre, Ms. Sterling recalled, advocated the abolishment of capital punishment in his doctoral thesis. "Events made him change his mind," she said.

Ms. Sterling said she was not so sure the Italian Communists really want to share power under the present crisis situation, "given the almost total economic collapse of the country." Their leaders know that in that case, and should they really want to bring order in the Italian economy, the Communists will have "to muzzle the working class . . . they must use the whip, tell the workers that absenteeism will be punishable." They will have "to introduce a wage freeze, impose a 30 percent tax on every bank account over ten million lire, and an efficient system to make the rich pay their taxes."

The working class, "the most militant one in Europe, determined to destroy the capitalist system, which is not what the Communists are trying to do," will strongly resist such "muzzling," Ms. Sterling explained. Moreover, she went on, the workers "will ask the Party: 'what are you fellows waiting for? who is stopping you? why aren't you barging in and carrying out the fundamental Communist program?'"

If the Communist Party does not act according to these demands, "it will be faced with the alternative of either leaving the government in disgrace, or doing what Berlinguer says he abhors, which is resort to the scalpel," she said.

The Communists and NATO

Discussing in conclusion the Communist Party's foreign policy, Ms. Sterling said it was true that Berlinguer has repeatedly stated that he would not oppose continued Italian membership in the Atlantic Alliance, but a *L'Unita* editorial stressed that it was wrong to believe that the Communists "could accept the Atlantic pact as it is" because it is, according to the Party's official organ, "one of the fundamental instruments of American manipulation of the politics and economics of our own country and of all of Western Europe."

While the Italian Communists, the editorial continued, acknowledge that NATO must exist as long as there is a Warsaw Pact on the other side, the Alliance itself must be "restructured to break the American hegemony, permitting the European members to reestablish their sovereignty."

What *L'Unita* was in fact saying, Ms. Sterling said, was that "the Americans should be driven out of NATO, or that the American public should be so provoked by the attitude of the NATO allies that it would demand the withdrawal of the atomic umbrella from Europe."

Some Provocative Questions

In a question-and-answer period following the presentations by the panelists, former White House aide Jack Valenti, now president of the Motion Picture Association of America, asked whether he understood Ms. Sterling as saying that the Italian Christian Democrats were "really inept," and also whether a Communist takeover was "inevitable."

"There is no evidence that they are aware of the urgency of the problem or for the need for them [the Christian Democrats] to totally change the kind of leadership they provided for the last 30 years," Ms. Sterling replied. Concerning the Communist Party, she said she believed "they will try to avoid" the takeover because "they are terrified of the possibility of an open confrontation if they go too far." Also, she cautioned, "it is not absolutely sure that the Communists will win the next elections and become the first party." But, she added, whatever the outcome of the next elections, it is "no more possible to say: never mind, Italy has been around for 3,000 years, it will always be here, it will muddle through somehow."

Italians, she explained, are "in such a state of frustration, of anger and rancor that even if they scrape through the elections, it will not solve the problem of keeping the Communists out of power, and we will not keep them out by simply saying we don't want them there. A total new vocabulary is required in the United States to deal with this problem."

Chairman Connally reminded Ms. Sterling that the Christian Democrats held their party congress recently. "I assume the statements you made about the hopelessness of the [Christian Democratic] leadership still obtain, even after the congress. Nothing was done there to give new hope?" he asked.

An "Argentine Solution"?

Thomas Corcoran, veteran Washington lawyer and "brain-truster" of the

Roosevelt era asked whether the gloomy picture depicted by Ms. Sterling would indicate that there might be "an Argentine solution to the Italian problem," meaning a military takeover.

"I think there would be no worse disaster for Italy than an Argentine solution. It would immediately mean civil war. It would not work: the Communist Party is simply too powerful, and if there is a military takeover the party would find arms. There would be plenty of sources, one possibly Yugoslavia, which is frightened of a Communist government in Italy but would certainly not stand by if a military junta would take over," Ms. Sterling replied.

Colby said he could not share Ms. Sterling's views on the inevitability of a Communist takeover. The reason he thinks the "catastrophe she predicts can be avoided" is exactly what Ms. Sterling explained: "the Communist leadership is frightened by its worker base, is frightened of a premature bid for power and of being in a responsible position because of possible repudiation by its own members." At the same time, Colby said, the Christian Democrats will be extremely cautious and avoid fraternizing with the right, afraid of "generating a reaction from the left." Therefore, the former intelligence chief declared, "I believe you will see rather than a catastrophe of a left-wing dictatorship with a scalpel, or an Argentine-type military dictatorship, a continued struggle down these unpleasant alternatives with the now ruling parties rejecting the right, as they have done on several occasions, and dealing with the Communist Party, which has to yield to keep the structure going."

This, Colby acknowledged, is a "totally unsatisfactory solution for those who want neat political solutions, but it really is a reflection of the Italian genius for working through absolutely impossible situations, avoiding the ultimate failure of going toward a right- or left-wing dictatorship."

Degree of Soviet Influence?

Professor Joan Urban of Catholic University in a statement from the floor said that a careful reading of the Italian Communist press provides evidence of the Communist Party's growing independence from Moscow. Some of these papers, she said, "now attack the Soviet Union for the absence of liberty, they accuse some leaders in Moscow of being more Stalinists than Stalin was.

"This is most important," she declared. The Italian Communists go even so far that they defend the Spanish Communist Party which "almost broke with Moscow and is barely on speaking terms" with the Soviets. "We cannot rule out the possibility of a final break between Moscow and the PCI [Italian Communist Party] and it might happen that the party will change its relationship to Moscow in a radical fashion," she declared.

Colby replied with a word of caution. True, he said, that there is now polycentrism in the Communist world, but this reflects the present situation, especially "the absence of cold war, and a relatively good overall world economic situation."

"If you change some of these fundamentals, you can expect some changes in the policies, too, and the recognition that the link to the Soviet Union is still an essential element of Communist belief in dogma and ideology."

Professor Urban said in reply to Colby that "China was able to break that link to Moscow." Also she reminded him that Italian Communists already proved that they were not totally subservient to Moscow when Palmiro Togliatti was their leader. "There was conflict between Stalin and Togliatti. Togliatti has saved the life of [Marxist philospher Gyoergy] Lukacs of Hungary and the lives of a number of other leading Central European communists."

Dr. Cline said he thought Professor Urban neglected an important fact: that China split with the Soviets ten years after Mao Tse-tung reached "uncontested power." While it is "theoretically possible" that the Italian Communists, as Professor Urban predicted, might break with Moscow, "it seems to me much more likely that the Italian Communist Party will be under great pressure to hold its own and will be for a long time wanting as much help from Moscow as it can get," Dr. Cline said.

Chairman Connally also disagreed with Professor Urban. "Given the proximity and availability of [Soviet] resources nearby Italy, they [the Soviets] might well view the Italian Communists in a vastly different light from what they view the 800 million Chinese," he said.

Ms. Sterling said that while she would view Professor Urban's prediction as a "most interesting possibility," she found recently "disturbing indications of regression rather than advance in this field." Berlinguer's speech at the Moscow 25th Party Congress contained no new elements, "he did not say anything about Czechoslovakia. The Italian Communists stopped calling it an invasion, they are calling it a 'happening.' He [Berlinguer] did not mention any of the cultural freedom questions in the Soviet Union," Ms. Sterling said.

To illustrate her point she recalled Soviet Foreign Minister Andrey Gromyko's visit to Rome on the eve of the Helsinki conference on European security. Gromyko, she explained, came to the Italian capital "to lean on the Italians to take a position [in Helsinki] helpful to the Russians." When the Italian government leaders [the Christian Democrats] "refused to accept the Soviet position on the so-called Basket Three issues on human rights, the Russians called in Berlinguer. What Berlinguer should have done was to persuade Gromyko to take the Italian position. He was doing just the opposite, he was defending the Soviet views."

What Role for the U.S.?

Mrs. Anna Chennault said that after Vietnam the question is raised, especially in Asia, "What is the United States going to do? This question is asked by those who do not want Communist domination yet recognize the realities." Such reality is, she declared, that "While the Communists march, the whole world is asleep."

Admiral Rivero answered that not everyone recognizes the problem. "Many people think that everything is fine in relations with the Communists, so why rock the boat?" he said.

Colby, also replying to Mrs. Chennault, defended CIA assistance to those who were ready to fight Communist subversion. This, he stressed, "was not bribery . . . (and) we won the fight.

"This arm of our national arsenal must remain available to us, it must be carefully used, must be used in terms of a policy on which we Americans can agree upon, but we must not foreswear that kind of help to friends in foreign countries because it is sometimes very useful to avoid more critical situations," the former CIA director declared. But, he warned, such assistance must be given "according to our laws and our Consitution."

Ms. Sterling said that while she agreed with Colby "in a general way," she urged utmost caution.

"It is utterly essential in this age to make a distinction, to define what we are trying to stop," she said, "not socialism, not people's revolutionary movements which, they hope, rightly or wrongly, will mean a better economic and social life for them. What we should try to stop is the military, international threat to the security of the free world. This distinction is most important when we are talking about handing out money, because it does not mean just supporting any old buddy. Nothing could sound more wrong to European ears today."

West European Pressures

Former Deputy Undersecretary of State Nathaniel Samuels reminded the conference that in Portugal the European Socialists helped to prevent a Communist takeover. What is the European Community doing "to prevent the disaster described as being virtually inevitable" in Italy? Or must the United States" do something of a very drastic and dramatic nature" to prop up the ruling parties in that country, Samuels asked. "Should the United States take the initiative at this stage?" he said, adding that "at this moment Italy lacks confidence that the United States would irrevocably stand behind that country."

Replying to Samuels, Ms. Sterling said that there is a considerable difference between the situation in Portugal and that in Italy. "The Portuguese Communist Party was odious; it behaved badly. Cunhal [the leader of Portugal's Communists] behaved like a Stalinist; he was grabby, using violence, and the Socialists got up all over Europe to come to the defense of their comrades in Portugal. The Italian Communists are incapable of such grossly vulgar behavior and this affects the way Europe looks upon the Italian scene."

In answer to Samuels' direct question, Ms. Sterling said she believes "this is an excellent moment to work out an Atlantic Alliance form of rescue" in Italy. The Germans, she noted, are ready "for some sort of mutual action in this field," but added that "the United States has a great deal to do to overcome its past sins in its relationship with its European allies; we must find a new way of working with them."

Chairman Connally said that the United States, through the World Bank and the International Monetary Fund, "is working in concert with other nations in trying to solve economic, social and structural problems in many areas of the world."

What is Appropriate U.S. Reaction?

A staff member of the House Committee on International Relations, Peter Abbruzzese, said in remarks from the floor that Congress has only limited powers in forming foreign policy. Regarding the specific question of Italy he said he was "not sure how much we can do, and whether we should do it."

In a brief reply Chairman Connally said he was "grateful for the admission that Congress cannot run the foreign policy of this country."

Another participant said he frequently was asked the question in Italy how the United States can protect that country when it tolerates Communism some 80 miles off its shores, an obvious reference to Cuba.

"This question does arise in many parts of the world," Colby replied. "Once people thought America can do everything without limits . . . Of course we can't do everything, but we can do many things; the problem is to define the right tool for the right situation.

"There have been situations in which we used the wrong tools, we made errors, like in the Bay of Pigs when it was thought that the people of Cuba would arise and they didn't. There was an error involved in the estimate, but the answer is not that the Bay of Pigs was impossible, the answer would be to work for another two or three years on the political background so that the estimate that they [the Cubans] would rise would be accurate," the former intelligence chief declared.

"Once we have reestablished self-confidence we will face these problems with a greater degree of subtlety than we have in the past," Colby said.

An Italian newsman asked from the floor what were the political consequences which the United States could accept if the Mediterranean, as Admiral Rivero said, became a Soviet lake?

Chairman Connally recalled that the U.S. administration has said Communist participation in the Italian government "would be unacceptable, whatever that means." Colby said his concern was that the people of the Mediterranean area would "make compromises with the rising Soviet imperialistic Communist power" and that their loyalty to NATO would weaken. Admiral Rivero reiterated that the neutralization of Italy "would promote the neutralization of Greece and Turkey, the war against [Soviet] submarines would become extremely difficult and the Warsaw Pact could divert all its resources to the center front" of Europe.

Jenonne Walker of the State Department insisted that Secretary of State Henry Kissinger did not say that Communist participation in the Italian government would be "unacceptable . . . he made no threats and did not say what the United States would do if it happened." The question is, she said, "what would be the PCI's behavior in a coalition? Would they acquiesce in Italy's participation in NATO?"

The Italian Communists, Ms. Sterling said, "never made much mileage on foreign policy issues: that is not what wins the Italian voter." The Italian Communist Party "could go on avoiding . . . foreign policy issues . . . . What makes them terribly nervous is the relationship between the United States and the Soviet Union."

Another question which remains unanswered, she went on, is what the effects would be in Eastern Europe of a Communist takeover or participation in the Italian government. This begins to be an awful problem for the Russians . . . There is no question about it that the Russians would go to war if anything threatened their Eastern European empire . . . . and if the Communists go too far in Italy and arouse too much envy and unrest in Eastern Europe, this could create an alarming situation for the Russians."

Colby said he agreed that the question to be answered was whether the Communists could participate in governing Italy without touching on international problems. Therefore, he said. "I insist that one of the fundamentals is the détente atmosphere." Had the Communists been in the Italian government in October 1973, they would have had a "a terrible time" confronted with the American alert ordered during the new round of the Middle East War. Such things might happen again and they would "automatically put the Communists into a terrible position."

Dr. Penelope Hartland-Thunberg, Director of Economic Research at CSIS, asked what impact it would have in Italy if the President accepted the recommendation of the International Trade Commission to raise the duty on imported shoes in view of the fact that one third of this import comes from Italy.

"Utterly appalling," Ms. Sterling replied.

In a statement from the floor a member of the U.S. Army said that Communist participation in the Italian government would be "unfortunate, but not catastrophic." Should it happen, he said, "the Communists will be as concerned about internal stability as are the Christian Democrats. The Communists need the support of the workers, but also of the Italian populace at large; they need the support of the Europeans and that of the United States.

"We must deal with this possibility on an even keel. The rhetoric we have heard has not been really productive and has created a schism in the European Community."

The United States, he suggested, should not take the initiative but "promote an Italian and European solution" and "differentiate between Italian and U.S. interests because they are not necessarily convergent."

Conference Report

Evening Session

After an introduction by Conference Chairman Connally, former Ambassador to Italy Clare Boothe Luce delivered the keynote speech, a sharp critique of current U.S. foreign policy.

Détente vs. Containment

Mrs. Luce was especially critical of détente. No other foreign policy principle "has ever been harder to come to grips with, or caused so much semantic confusion," she said.

There was no such problem with the earlier East-West policy of containment, Mrs. Luce declared. "It was America's global response to the global threat of world revolutionary Communism. Unlike détente—the word just won't go away—the word containment was a wonderfully unambiguous word . . . . Every American and every foreigner knew not only what containment meant, but who and what was to be contained. There was no confusion anywhere about the policy's objective. It was to prevent the ideological and military expansion of totalitarianism into the non-Communist or free world, by peaceful or cold war methods if possible, by hot war if Communist aggression made it necessary."

Containment, she said, was "both an idealistic and realistic policy. It was designed to meet the Communist global challenge at every level: military, political, and ideological."

This policy, Mrs. Luce explained, not only rehabilitated the economies of the three major World War II enemies: those of Japan, Germany, and Italy, but "thanks to containment and its creation of NATO, there has been no war in Europe for 30 years, the longest period of peace Europe has known in its entire history."

History, she said, "will certainly not view containment as an unsound policy. It did not fail us. We failed it."

When the "long, ill-conceived, badly fought war" in Vietnam eroded the consensus for containment, a "dangerous vacuum" was created in U.S. foreign policy. This vacuum was filled in 1972 by détente. "It might be more accurate to say that it was filled by Dr. Kissinger and his shuttle diplomacy," Mrs. Luce asserted.

The results of détente were poor, she said. She mentioned the Soviet and Cuban presence in Angola, the Syrian move into Lebanon, the Palestine Liberation Organization (PLO) which "has become a Soviet client," and continued turmoil in the Middle East.

Additional negative results of détente are the growing Soviet strength in Central and Eastern Europe, "the North Koreans are itching to go, India has passed into the Soviet orbit . . . (and) the dominoes are still falling in Southeast Asia."

In Europe, she continued, Portugal, a member of NATO, "is not yet safely off the democratic danger list; Cyprus and Turkey have not yet composed their differences . . . NATO is in a state of shocking disarray."

Finally, Italy is on the verge of the "historic compromise," the possibility of Communist participation in that country's government.

New U.S. Policy Needed

Although President Ford has ordered that the word détente should be dropped from the diplomatic vocabulary and replaced by the term "peace through strength," the vacuum continues to exist and "if it is not soon filled by a policy addressed to the international realities, will lead on the Soviet Installment Plan to the isolation of America." Mrs. Luce declared.

She said:

"There would be no Italian Communist problem if there were no Soviet Union . . . . There would be no Italian Communist problem if the Italian people did not feel that the United States has no policy today that promises them any hope that they will not, in the end, be relentlessly drawn into the orbit of Moscow."

Kissinger, Mrs. Luce recalled, warned European leaders that an Italian Communist role in the government "could have a political domino effect in France and in West Germany which would lead to the withdrawal of American forces" from those countries. Therefore, she quoted Kissinger as arguing, the United States would oppose the "historic compromise" with Communism in Italy as long as possible, though it must deal with Communists after they came to power.

"Considering that our dealings with the Soviets have been wonderfully generous . . . it is not surprising that many Italians feel that Italy might derive more economic and political consideration from the United States if Italy did become a Communist power," she said.

Italy's best hope for a prosperous economy and for maintaining democracy depends on that country's continued membership in the family of Western European nations. But, Mrs. Luce said, "there is no question where they [the Italians] would stand if push came to shove and the Soviets achieved domination of the Mediterranean. Also, there is no question that this is precisely what the USSR intends to do. In fact there is now only one open question: do the American people, or do they not, have the will to resist Soviet imperialism?"

This question, she declared, will be answered next fall when the new President is elected, "whoever he may be."

"It will be revealed to us in the foreign policy stand taken by the winning candidate. For no candidate is going to win unless his foreign policy views reflect the will of the people."

Concluding on a more optimistic note Mrs. Luce said she was convinced that the American people "are recovering from the trauma of Vietnam and are once again preparing themselves to shoulder the task of world leadership.

"We are the richest, the strongest, the freest nation in the world. If it is not our destiny to be the guardian of freedom in what is left of the free world, whose destiny is it?" she asked.

What Should the U.S. Do?

After Mrs. Luce's address, Chairman Connally invited questions from the floor.

Thomas Corcoran said that both major political parties in the United States are on the record with their determination to defend Israel's integrity. How can this be done if the situation in the Mediterranean is so grave as depicted by some of the panelists, he asked.

It was "nip and tuck" the last time [meaning the 1973 war], Mrs. Luce replied. "We cannot let the key to the Mediterranean, which is Italy, fall out of our grasp."

Colby said the task is to find some "subtle technique" which would permit the United States to avoid the "terrible alternatives: either a major war or defeat." Several interim steps could be taken before the Communists would control Italy and these steps would help "to avoid the ultimate question ever being raised, avoid military confrontation."

The question is whether the interim steps Colby suggested "can be taken in time." Ms. Sterling asked. Would they prevent the neutralization of Italy? Then she asked Mrs. Luce to tell how American aid given to Italy was used.

19

"Much of the aid was misused by the Christian Democrats, but this is no good reason for our turning the key over to the Communists," Mrs. Luce replied. Then she was asked from the floor what Americans could do to help the Italians in their present quandary?

After the war, she recalled, Americans of Italian descent "pitched in." They told their kin in Italy: "Look fellows, stick with us, don't make the big mistake" of voting for the Communists. "Now is the time for another people-to-people campaign. This is what American-Italians should do," she suggested.

Connally endorsed Mrs. Luce's proposal. There are 22 million American-Italians, and almost 50 million Catholics in this country, he said. "They know that one of the Communist objectives is to control Catholicism."

Returning to Corcoran's question, Connally said that "Israel's front line defense is Italy" and this defense depends on the free flow of oil from the Middle East. "If indeed Israel is in jeopardy because of the fall of Italy, then indeed the oil fields of the Middle East are even more in danger and the entire economic vitality of the free world is in jeopardy," Connally said.

Dan Gilmore of United Press International asked how a newsman should explain that friendly relations with the Soviet Union or with China "are all right while saying that Communist takeover in Italy is unacceptable?"

"There is a growing awareness in America that détente is dead, though not yet officially buried," Mrs. Luce replied. "Something is stirring in the American people, call it if you want nationalism. Americans are suddenly beginning to sense that no nation, not even America, can stand alone. They will understand that the key to the Atlantic Alliance is Italy."

Defining U.S. Policy Toward Italy

Professor Stanislaw Wasowski of Georgetown University asked what the proper U.S. policy toward Italy should be?

"A special policy is impossible except in the context of policy toward the West and toward Europe. When we have it, our policy toward Italy will fall right into place. We haven't got it yet, but we are going to have one," Mrs. Luce answered.

"There is one word for such policy: friendship," Colby remarked.

Friendship, Ms. Sterling added, means "comprehension of Italy's needs. Friendship can become an almost meaningless phrase if it does not show the comprehension of immediate, very real needs."

Dale Herspring of the State Department complained that the conference neglected the question of the relationship between the Italian Communist Party and the Soviet Union. It is a "bit naive" to believe that "everything is concentrated in Moscow. In Italy the Soviets are getting into a very nasty corner," Herspring said.

"The Soviets have a state and a party interest in what is happening in Western Europe," Colby replied. He said:

"They [the Soviets] are conducting a two-level diplomacy. They are having a little trouble with the party level nowadays because of the détente situation on the state level. But if the situation becomes more severe, more serious on the state level, then the discipline on the party level will sharpen up considerably and you will see the strengthening of the ties between the Communist Party of the Soviet Union and the Communist Party of Italy."

Endre Marton
Rapporteur

Background Paper

The Mediterranean and Italy:
Global Context of a Local Problem

by Dr. Wynfred Joshua*, Defense Intelligence Agency

Not since the creation of the North Atlantic Alliance in the late 1940s have such disturbing questions been raised about the continued viability of the Western defense posture. Critics of SALT warn that another agreement threatens to codify Soviet strategic advantages. A recent study of the Library of Congress on the military capabilities of the superpowers points to a stark shift in the global balance of power unfavorable to the West.[1] In the halls of the U.S. Congress and other forums the question is debated as to whether the Soviet Union is outspending the U.S. in the military sector. More important than weapons and financial statistics, however, are the doubts cast on the American will that has nurtured the Western Alliance system since its inception. The collapse of more than a decade of U.S. commitment and endeavor in Vietnam has widely been interpreted in U.S. and allied circles as a neo-isolationist retreat. Publicity surrounding the Congressional intelligence investigations has compounded the concern at home and abroad that there may be a permanent impairment of U.S. resolve, rather than a passing trauma.

The Cassandras are no longer confined to the members of the Western defense establishments entrusted with the security of their countries. In Western media and academic circles a kind of Spenglerian vision is being articulated of a West in decline faced by a virile and confident barbarian of the Soviet imperium. Perhaps nowhere is the threat to the Western Alliance more sharply drawn than at NATO's southern flank where military and political trends combine to present a profound challenge to the defense of the West.

Militarily the changing balance of power in southern Europe is most clearly reflected in the Soviet naval presence in the Mediterranean. Started in the early sixties, the Soviet naval buildup has been most noticeable in the 1967

*Dr. Joshua is a Defense Intelligence Officer at the Defense Intelligence Agency, Department of Defense. The views and conclusions in this paper are solely those of the author.

[1]John M. Collins, *The United States/Soviet Military Balance* (Washington: Library of Congress, 1976).

and 1973 Arab-Israeli wars. Yet the implications of the Soviet Mediterranean squadron transcend the military impact and should be gauged in political terms for it affects the political climate of the littoral countries as well.

Contributing to the erosion of the political-military posture at the eastern end of the Mediterranean are the differences over Cyprus among the U.S., Greece, and Turkey. The subsequent suspension of U.S. operations at Turkish facilities and Greece's withdrawal from NATO's integrated command structure have shaken the political cohesion and military preparedness of the southern flank. Unfortunately, the intractable Cyprus affair remains the obstacle to repairing the strained relations between Turkey and Greece and their NATO allies.

Along the eastern and southern shores of the Mediterranean from Lebanon to Morocco the countries are troubled by radical Arab fervor, frequently fanned by Palestinian activists, and by rival territorial claims, often linked with generous economic prizes as in the case of the Spanish Sahara. By exploiting the divergencies between radical and traditional regimes and by championing the Arab cause in the Arab-Israeli conflict, the Soviets have sought to cultivate Arab leaders. Israel and Egypt for obvious reasons aside, Soviet activities have generally increased in the North African and eastern Mediterranean. Admittedly, Soviet leverage remains at best an uncertain commodity. Yet the pro-Western stance that once prevailed in this sector of the Mediterranean region has largely dissipated.

Across the northwestern rim of the Mediterranean the situation is somewhat less bleak. Portugal has for the time being shed the threat of a Communist takeover which hovered over it for much of 1975. But Lisbon's virgin democratic adventure is still facing problems because of the continued political disarray, factionalization in the military, and soaring economic difficulties. In its Iberian neighbor there are prospects for the establishment of a viable pro-Western government notwithstanding the strains which a transition from an authoritarian regime to a more open system inevitably engenders. The proposed U.S.-Spanish friendship treaty, moreover, will draw Spain closer into the Western defense system. This relationship will clearly strengthen the troubled southern flank. Spanish entry into the NATO club, however, remains remote in view of the opposition of some NATO members who have yet to pardon Spain for its Franquist past.

In the center of the southern flank, the spectre that the Italian and French Communist Parties are moving toward national political office is fueling growing concern in Western councils. If Communists were to gain power in Italy, the French Communist Party, which already seeks to emulate its Italian counterpart in several respects, would be greatly encouraged.

Whereas in other parts of the Mediterranean Western diplomacy may be able to alleviate some of the troubles, in Italy the situation is more complicated. The problem in Italy inheres in the weakness of the economic and political institutions. This is reflected in the rivalry between an aging Christian Democratic majority party, rent with scandal and divisions, and a growing and disciplined Communist Party, seeking to convey an image of integrity and national independence. The issue that occupies the attention of NATO leaders is what the possible consequences would be if the Communists were to join the government in Rome. Just posing this question risks raising a self-fulfilling prophecy. Yet in light of the interest this issue has fanned at home and abroad, it appears appropriate to review the role of NATO's Mediterranean flank in the Western defense and the significance of Italian political instability within this broader strategic context.

The Superpowers in the Mediterranean

The strategic significance of the Mediterranean has been obvious for centuries. It remains the most traversed maritime area in the world. It flanks the European landmass at the south. It provides access to the shortest water route from Europe to the Persian Gulf and beyond. It forms the bridge between three continents; and via the Black Sea it probes deep into the southern heartland of Eurasia.

U.S. Interests

Initially, the introduction of a permanent U.S. presence in the region in 1947 was designed to replace fading British and French power and to contain the Soviet Union. The conviction that a secure Mediterranean flank was vital to the political and territorial integrity of Western Europe inspired U.S. policy from the start. With the advent of the NATO alliance the Mediterranean basin and environs assumed increasing strategic importance for the U.S. The region hosted the military bases essential to maintain the strategic deterrent and provided an area from which U.S. air and naval power could be brought to bear in defense of the European theater. Furthermore, the tangible evidence of the U.S. commitment as manifested by the presence of the Sixth Fleet and the network of American bases in the Mediterranean helped to sustain the resilience of the southern NATO members against Soviet pressures. This was particularly so for Turkey and Greece for whom NATO's security umbrella was largely synonymous with that of the U.S. Neither Ankara nor Athens entertained any illusions that the West European members would rally to their defense when necessary, let alone that they would help each other.

There was, moreover, in the broader Mediterranean-Middle East area a less easily articulated U.S. concern for protecting Western interests against the Soviet Union, but it clearly included the protection of access to Middle East oil resources. U.S. interests in the region would therefore be served by stability and a political solution to the Arab-Israeli conflict.

The insertion of Soviet political influence and military forces in the Mediterranean added another factor to the rationale for the U.S. presence and policy. Through the Mediterranean run the lifelines of NATO's southern members. Washington sought therefore to prevent its Soviet opponent from becoming the ascendant power in the region and to deny Moscow military superiority that could be translated into tactical advantages and political gains.

Soviet Interests

From a vantage point in Moscow, the Mediterranean region with its strategic character has been a target since the days of Peter the Great. The need to protect Russia's southern borders and the ambitions of the Czars to expand southwards have traditionally been reflected in the effort to dominate the countries near or adjacent to Russia's southern flank. Turkish control over the Bosporus, the Sea of Marmara, and the Dardanelles have limited the utility of Russian Black Sea ports and restricted the flexibility of the Russian Black Sea Fleet. Control of the Turkish Straits, penetration into the Mediterranean, and access to warm water ports on an open sea are considerations that have for centuries infused Russian Mediterranean policies.

The remnants of Czarist aspirations, however, do not suffice to explain contemporary Soviet concerns. Soviet policies are also formulated within an ideological framework and in a coordinated fashion toward the achievement of fundamental Soviet goals. Within this broader context the neutralization of Western Europe and the creation of a climate receptive to Soviet interests remain basic Soviet objectives. While these goals are clearly reserved for the longer term, Soviet ascendancy over the Mediterranean region would bring this within Moscow's reach, for Europe would be outflanked from the south. As a less ambitious step the Soviets sought, therefore, to end Western hegemony in the southern region and to change the political climate into one with a neutralist cast. With some 95 Soviet ships in the Mediterranean during the October 1973 war—a number substantially larger than that of the Sixth Fleet—the first part has long been achieved.

Soviet interests in the waterways and watermasses around the Mediterranean fit into Soviet global maritime pretentions. Originally Soviet strategists saw the role of the Soviet navy as protecting the homeland and as an adjunct to the ground forces. Since the 1960s they have stressed the need to project

Soviet power and political reach throughout the world through the visible presence of the Soviet fleet. The multi-ocean OKEAN exercises of the Soviet navy amply demonstrate Soviet worldwide maritime strategy. The more immediate and local Soviet interests in the Mediterranean aside, Soviet naval intrusion in the region helps to consumate this broader naval strategy.

In addition about half of the Soviet merchant marine vessels operate from Black Sea ports and ply the Mediterranean to ports throughout the world. The visits of Soviet merchant and naval ships to Mediterranean ports help to create a psychological impact on the littoral states by reminding them that the Soviet Union is not a distant power, but present at their shores.

Beyond strategic and ideological considerations Moscow has a more practical interest in the Mediterranean inasmuch as it includes the oil routes from the Middle East. The Soviets sharply recognize the importance of Middle East oil resources for the West; the threat of interruption of the oil flow to NATO Europe would drastically reduce the range of options open to the Alliance in a crisis or war. Already long before the October 1973 war did the Soviets urge the Arabs to use oil as an instrument of coercion against the West. Furthermore, looking toward the 1980s, the Soviets are likely to need Middle East oil for their own consumption and for supplies to Eastern Europe. While estimates of Soviet oil requirements in the long term vary, most projections indicate that Soviet domestic consumption is expected to outrun Soviet production within the next decade. The USSR also provides half of East European oil needs, which are expected to rise substantially in the coming years. Soviet control or influence over these oil supplies would be a powerful lever to retain Moscow's sway over Eastern Europe. For all these reasons access to the oil resources of the Middle East have added a major dimension to Soviet concerns with the Mediterranean region.

In capsule form, a combination of historical aspiration, ideological imperatives, strategic considerations, and pragmatic calculations account for enduring Soviet interests in the Mediterranean. Of late few regions have offered the Soviets so many opportunities for furthering their objectives as Southern Europe has, torn as it is by divergent internal political and social forces. The Soviets have sought to take advantage of the problems at Europe's southern borders, as their overtures to Turkey suggest. But their policies have been carefully calculated to avoid initiatives that might produce a reaction inimical to their objectives or galvanize the West into a greater concerted defense effort. From a vantage point of the Southern European countries, however, Soviet political moves are intimately connected with the Soviet naval presence in the Mediterranean for this interacts directly with the political developments in the flank.

The Naval Instruments

As a rule the Soviets deploy close to 50 ships in the Mediterranean region, slightly more than the number of ships of the Sixth Fleet. In a crisis, however, the Soviets can quickly expand their naval forces as they did during the October 1973 war when they had about 95 ships in the Mediterranean in contrast with some 70 American ships there at the time. The concentration of Soviet naval forces at the eastern end of the Mediterranean has reduced the freedom of maneuver of the Sixth Fleet in that sector. Yet numbers alone do not tell the whole story. The two naval forces have different missions and capabilities. The U.S. Navy uses concentrated offensive fighting power and sophisticated amphibious tactics for projecting U.S. power. The Soviet Mediterranean squadron still reflects its original mission of neutralizing its American counterpart through emphasizing an attack submarine and a surface-to-surface missile capability. Furthermore, the U.S. is clearly superior in tactical air power which is critical to the control of the region. The Soviet naval presence is supported neither by sea-based aircraft which the U.S. carriers offer the Sixth Fleet, nor by the aircover that land-based aircraft could provide. Even before the deterioration in Soviet-Egyptian relations, the USSR lacked sufficient aircover for anything beyond two-thirds of the eastern basin of the Mediterranean.

The Soviets have sought to compensate for their lack of tactical air power with ship-based surface-to-surface and surface-to-air missile capabilities. Even if the new Soviet aircraft carrier with vertical/short take-off and landing aircraft, the *Kiev*, is deployed in the Mediterranean, Soviet aircover would not be appreciably enhanced. The balance of forces in the region will not have tilted against the West. A major variable in Soviet as well as Western calculations of the constellation of power remains the perception of the U.S. will to use the forces. At this stage Soviet policies do not suggest a perception in Moscow of a faltering of U.S. political resolve to defend U.S. interests in the Mediterranean and Europe. Nevertheless with questions raised in Washington and other Western capitals about continued American national will, it is crucial that the Soviets do not receive the wrong message. As a minimum the U.S. should retain its military presence in the region and support the pro-Western forces in the littoral lest Moscow get the impression that America is indeed retreating from its forward positions.

Italy's Role in Western Defense

Strategically, the defense of Europe's southern rim begins in the Atlantic. Hence the significance of the Iberian Atlantic Command in Lisbon and the joint U.S.-Spanish base at Rota, Spain, from where the West guards the approaches to the Mediterranean. At the eastern end of the region Turkey is the cornerstone of the NATO posture by dint of its position athwart the exit from the Black Sea and its location facing the USSR and straddling Soviet routes to the Middle East. As important as the NATO bases and installations at the western and eastern gates to the Mediterranean are, without Italy the Western defense posture in the region would be very difficult.

The establishment at Naples of the headquarters of the Allied Forces Southern Europe with its elaborate command, control, and communications network and its subordinate land, air, and naval commands attests to the central strategic role Italy plays in the defense of the southern European theater. Its position astride the center of the Mediterranean bestows upon Italy a critical strategic value. With its control over the narrow bottleneck between Sicily, Malta, and Cape Bon in Tunisia, the Italian peninsula and its Sicilian extension form in effect a gate across the Mediterranean. From Italian airbases the entire Mediterranean can be covered. Without Italian real estate the Mediterranean defense structure, which is basically a combined sea-air-land operation, would be significantly degraded.

Italy's territory is not merely important for the control of the Mediterranean region; it also provides a geographical backup area as well as dispersal sites for tactical airpower for the central European region. Together with France and the Iberian Peninsula Italy lends depth to the defense of the European theater.

The strategic concern of the NATO allies is not solely Italian membership in the Alliance; it is also the active participation of Italy in Western operations. Italy's role as the key to the defense of the Mediterranean is reflected in the extensive network of NATO facilities and U.S. forces stationed in Italy. Alone, the U.S. has some 11,000 military personnel and about 18,000 civilians, including between 16,000 and 17,000 dependents there. Naples is the home port of the Sixth Fleet and the site of naval air and naval support activity. Heavy naval maintenance of the Sixth Fleet is performed in Naples. Another naval support facility is at La Maddalena on Sardinia. U.S. maritime patrol aircraft are deployed from Sigonella on Sicily and Gaeta on the Italian peninsula.

Beyond offering its strategic real estate Italy's armed forces buttress the Western defense posture in the Mediterranean. There is a certain duality in Italy's military role. Its land and tactical airpower are organized for the defense of the homeland and are oriented toward fending off the threat from across the northeastern frontier. The Italian navy looks southward and focuses on the protection of the communication routes. The navy provides an important anti-submarine and anti-air warfare capability in local waters and constitutes a major combat presence in the Adriatic and Ionian Seas and the Sicilian Straits.

Less tangible, but equally important, is the contribution Italy renders to the political cohesion of the Alliance. Throughout NATO's history the division of Europe into a northern and southern sector has bedeviled the Alliance. Within Italy itself a similar north-south split, reinforced by economic differences, can be found. Much of the country, however, does not belong to the *Mezzogiorno*, i.e., the south, where about 35% of the people live, but identifies with the industralized north and searches for a European vocation rather than a Mediterranean role. Yet within the Alliance Italy is regarded, and regards itself, largely as a Mediterranean nation. To the extent that Italy nevertheless sees its destiny with Western Europe, Italy has blunted the sharp edges of the north-south fissure in NATO. At the same time Italy's participation as a Mediterranean member has helped to mitigate the fragmentation which afflicts the southern flank as a result of its geographical peculiarities and political diversity. Italy has thereby been part of the cement that has held the Alliance as well as the unruly southern region together.

Historic Compromise Communist Style

The success of the Italian Communist Party (PCI) in the regional elections of June 1975 took most political observers by surprise. The Communists came within 2 percentage points of becoming the largest party. The PCI scored an advantage of 5.5 percentage points, the greatest gain recorded by any political party in Italy since 1948. The electoral returns gave the PCI 33.4% of the vote; the Socialists (PSI) 12%; the Social Democrats 5.6%; while the Christian Democrats (DC), Italy's majority party, garnered 35.3% The outcome registered a widespread concern over Italy's persistent economic crisis as well as frustration with what was popularly perceived as the ineptitude and corruption of the Christian Democrats, who had dominated Italian politics for the last 30 years. It also starkly demonstrated the effectiveness of PCI tactics in portraying the party as a paradigm of efficiency and honesty, and independent from Moscow. Many non-Communists undoubtedly consoled themselves by claiming that the large Communist turnout was primarily a protest vote. Yet some 60% of the 18 year-olds and above who were voting for the first time had cast their ballot for the PCI.[2] This bespeaks major Communist inroads in the generation now coming of age in Italy rather than only an ephemeral protest vote. Italy's postwar history, moreover, has shown that general elections tend to hew closely to the trend established in local polling.

The Communists themselves have been pressing for an entente with the Catholics or the so-called historic compromise. Somewhat vaguely defined,

[2]*Newsweek*, June 30, 1975, p. 28.

there are different versions of the compromise, the essence of which amounts to a coalition of the Communists, the Christian Democrats and the Socialists. The PCI, however, has left no doubt that such an arrangement could only be consumated with a DC party which had undergone a "thorough revision and transformation of leadership."[3] Clearly the historic compromise would be the death knell of the DC as it currently exists; eventually the compromise Italian Communists style would be the PCI as the central dominating power with left-wing Christian Democrats and other left-wing forces in its orbit.

The Socialists, who supported the governing Moro coalition at the time of the June 1975 elections, became increasingly concerned that the two largest parties might arrive at an agreement which would relegate their party to obscure third-party status, if not leave it out in the cold altogether. They keenly felt that as long as the Communists were not associated with the national government, the latter would enjoy all the advantages of being an opposition party and escape the blame for the stringent measures the government would have to take for coping with the economic crisis. Yet, the Socialists acutely knew that by dint of their support of the Moro regime they would have to share responsibility for its policy. From a Socialist vantage point, the left-of-center formula with which Italy had been governed for the last 12 years had patently lost its validity. Within the Socialist party where the rank and file are more attracted by the seductive line of the Communists than by the inertia of the Christian Democrats, pressures mounted for an "alternative of the left," i.e., a popular front of the Socialists with the Communists. On the other hand, some key Socialist leaders, wary of taking the Communist plunge, held out for forging a special PSI-DC alliance which would run the country along Socialist lines. In any case, when the Moro coalition government refused to accept the Socialist program for economic reforms, but was nevertheless prepared to consult informally with the PCI on key questions, the Socialists in January 1976 withdrew their support from the government and brought down the Moro coalition.

The June 1975 fiasco had thrown the Christian Democrats into disarray. It also nudged the party perceptibly to the left. This was illustrated by the ouster of Party Secretary Amintore Fanfani, who was allied with the center and right-wing factions of the party, and the election instead of Benigno Zaccagnini, who was committed to the left-of-center factions. As a collection of disparate factions spanning the political spectrum from right to left, the DC has consistently lacked the unity of purpose to impose the economic, administrative, and social reforms Italy needed. Nor has the DC been able to overcome within the party

---

[3]*The Economist*, February 28, 1976, p. 54.

the generation gap between its entrenched aging leadership at the national level and its more aggressive, but less influential younger leaders on the local scene. The inability to cope with Italy's economic and social ills and the preoccupation with the distribution of patronage increasingly undermined the DC's power position and caused a rapid succession of coalition governments. When in early 1976 yet another coalition collapsed, the option of one more left-of-center arrangement vanished. Unable to enter with the Socialists into a special alliance, and opposed to the historic compromise, the DC formed a single-party minority government. It realized, however, that this could well force early general elections which otherwise could wait till May 1977.

Whether the present Moro government will prove to be any less ephemeral than its predecessors remains to be seen. As the sole governing party the DC will have to shoulder the burden for the reforms Italy badly needs or try to muddle through till the next election. In either case the DC is likely to incur the dissatisfaction of the electorate. Scenting national power, some Communist leaders have already threatened that they may resort to the "leftist alternative" if the Christian Democrats remain intransigent toward the historic compromise. The Socialists for their part have reiterated at their March 1976 National Congress their long-range goal of forming a coalition of left-wing forces once the PCI has clearly severed its Moscow connection.[4] The Social Democrats at their Congress in March 1976 have shifted drastically to the left and have adopted a posture which shows scant difference from that of the Communists. In short, if the pattern set by the June 1975 polling repeats itself at the next general election, the spectre of Communist participation in the government, if not a historic compromise Communist style, could become a reality.

Red Shadow Over Italy

Another spectacular Communist victory in the next elections is by no means a foregone conclusion. A marked upturn in Italy's economic fortunes or the rejuvenation of the Christian Democrats that would galvanize the party into action could reverse current political trends. The Italian electorate itself might have second thoughts and refuse to vote the Communists into power. If the PCI became nonetheless the majority party, the Socialists and other minority parties might still refuse to form with the PCI a left-wing front and throw their support behind the Christian Democrats. Nor is the historic compromise inevitable. Still with the Communists appearing on the crest of the hill, it is not unreasonable to explore the implications of Communist participation in the

---

[4]*The Economist,* March 13, 1976, p. 48.

government for Italy's defense effort and the broader Western defense posture in the Mediterranean.

Officially, the Italian Communists are on record that if they were to join the government they would abide by Italy's international commitments, including the NATO alliance until the "dissolution of the blocs." As an Italian scholar observed, "the real problem is not *whether* but *how* to stay" in NATO.[5] The PCI's position, however, has been carefully adopted for tactical purposes and is part of a broader effort to project a nationalist and democratic image of the party.

The PCI's rhetoric favoring "abolition of the blocs," is identical with Moscow's, and has the added advantage of avoiding the pitfalls of calling for unilateral Italian withdrawal from the Alliance. On virtually all foreign policy issues of note, particularly on East-West questions, the PCI has faithfully dovetailed the Soviet position. The major exceptions were the Soviet invasion of Czechoslovakia, some aspects of European integration, and the convening of a meeting of all European Communist Parties. The independent stance the PCI adopted, however, was largely aimed at audiences at home rather than what it purported to be—a serious attack on Moscow. Enrico Berlinguer, the present party leader who is identified with promoting the nationalist brand of Communism, has repeatedly stressed the PCI's "unbreakable ties of solidarity with Soviet Russia."[6] It is, moreover, not at all certain that once in the government, the PCI leadership would remain in the hands of Berlinguer and his allies. The more openly pro-Soviet wing of the Communists may well gain ascendancy and align Italy closely with the USSR.

Whichever leader or faction would dominate, the PCI is not likely to lose sight of its basic goals and programs which it has pressed for decades. These clearly do not include defense efforts. Even if Communist ministers would not be stage-managed by Moscow, they nevertheless profess little sympathy with NATO's values and objectives; they would try to cut defense budgets and Italy's military cooperation with NATO. This would undermine not only Italian defense, but the broader Western defense posture as well.

Assuming that Italy would opt to remain in NATO, would the U.S. and its allies not quickly encounter obstacles and delays in trying to use Italian bases and facilities? The predilection of the Italian bureaucracy to procrastinate is not unknown. Their reputation for efficiency notwithstanding, the Communists are likely to exploit this bureaucratic tendency for impeding the utilization of bases and installations on Italian soil. The entire network of facilities as well as

[5]Cesare Merlini, "Italy in the European Community and the Atlantic Alliance," *The World Today,* April 1975, p. 166.

[6]*Time*, March 15, 1976.

cooperation with U.S. and NATO allies in Italy would become hostage to Communist power.

Although at least initially Communist ministers in the Italian cabinet are likely to try to change little in Rome's foreign and defense policies, NATO itself would be faced with a formidable dilemma. When Portugal was led by the pro-Communist Vasco Goncalves regime, the Alliance already experienced serious problems in protecting classified data. But whereas Portugal in many respects remained on the periphery of NATO planning and operations and did not have large allied forces on its soil, Italy is in a different situation. In contrast with Portugal, Italy is at the center of NATO political and military planning and operations. It is a charter member of the Nuclear Planning Group in which the most sensitive issues of nuclear defense are discussed. Italy hosts a major NATO Command, with four of its subordinate commands. In short, the problems of safeguarding NATO plans and data against the Communists would be immense if not impossible.

A more philosophical but very real issue is the question of compatibility. Can a nation with Communists in its government remain in an alliance which has as its historical justification the defense of the Western democracies against the threat of Communist aggression? The PCI has few if any democratic traits; it operates on the basis of democratic centralism whereby decisions are imposed from the top. Like other Communist parties, it tolerates no meaningful dissent, but maintains iron discipline. The argument frequently advanced in Western Europe that the Communist Party of Italy has basically become a social democratic party is simply a delusion. If Italian Communists are really social democrats in disguise, could they not just as well have joined one of the social democratic parties rather than the PCI? The answer can be found in the fundamental differences between the Communists and social democrats.

In spite of the PCI's claim of honoring Italy's commitment to the Western Alliance, how far would its solidarity with NATO extend on East-West issues? In fact, the danger for Italy would be drifting into neutralism, thereby severely upsetting the balance of power in the Mediterranean.

Beyond the impact on Italy itself, the PCI's accession to national power would surely embolden other Communist parties in the southern littoral who profess a similar independent stance. Their domestic audiences may well be reassured by the example in Italy, where the Communists would be calculating enough to avoid pressing for drastic changes too soon. While the domino theory may not be applicable to every country in the flank, neutralism would soon cast its expanding shadow over southern Europe.

Reduced to bare essentials, Communists joining the Italian government would have profound implications. With some adjustments to allow for local conditions, Italy's domestic course would eventually be fashioned along the lines of an East European state. Rome's foreign policy orientation would undoubtedly undergo an equally far-reaching shift. The consequences for southern Europe and the Western defense in the Mediterranean are likely to come apace. An increasingly neutralist southern flank and a progressively deteriorating Western security posture would impose major restraints on the U.S. in the Mediterranean. The region's receptivity to Soviet pressures would grow as would its vulnerability to Soviet naval power. Without conspicuous efforts, the Soviet Union would truly have outflanked Europe from the south.

In light of these somber prospects, the risks to the West in permitting the Communists to come to power are too great to be tested. The U.S. and its allies, however, are not yet without any recourse; they may wish to consider a number of options.

The U.S. can take measures that attenuate the effects of Italy's economic recession. The attraction of the Communists for those who vote to register their protest would thereby be mitigated. The U.S. could extend generous loans to help shore up the faltering Italian economy. The lack of the most desirable collateral should not deter U.S. aid. After all, this is what alliances are all about. Furthermore, this is hardly the time to raise barriers against Italian imports. The rewards of derailing the Italian Communist momentum surely transcend the immediate gains of protecting American industries.

Among the left-of-center Christian Democrats, who have become increasingly vociferous of late, there is a widespread belief that the historic compromise would leave them unscathed and NATO undamaged. They should be under no misunderstanding as to what the consequences would be. It should be clear that neither the U.S. government nor its electorate could welcome Communist cabinet members in a country as central to the Alliance as Italy. So far the warnings of U.S. officials have not inspired much visible concern beyond the claim of Western interference in the domestic affairs of an ally. This attitude reflects partly the tarnished image and declining credibility of the U.S. For this reason, the private voices of the American establishment need to be raised.

Private and official West European leaders alike should be encouraged to impress the Italians with the implications of a drastic shift to the left. In many respects the West European allies may have more credibility in convincing Italian audiences of the disaster they are courting.

The U.S. should support those Italians who continue to be its friends. Though bruised by the unkind allegations in the Italian media about American aid, a great power does not abandon those who are its allies. The form and substance of U.S. support, however, should be left to the Italians.

Finally, the U.S. may wish to strengthen its military presence in the Mediterranean. Naval forces have the advantage that their limited visibility to the local populace incurs few political liabilities. Yet the message of continued U.S. political and military support is starkly conveyed.

Clearly, the future of the West in Italy is fraught with dangers. Much will depend on the Italian and U.S. will to stay the course. The prophets of doom notwithstanding, there is no reason yet to assume the relinquishment of Western resolve.

Background Paper

Political Crisis in Italy
by Marino de Medici
Correspondent for *Il Tempo*, Rome, Italy

Italy's seemingly infinite capacity to survive political and economic crises may have ended with the advent of 1976. And this time, more than ever before, some observers are saying, the only solution may be in the so-called "historic compromise," the sharing of power with Italy's Communist Party (PCI).

That prospect was enhanced on March 18, 1976, when Christian Democratic Prime Minister Aldo Moro held a 90-minute meeting with Communist Party leader Enrico Berlinguer. The Christian Democrats were quick to deny that the meeting signified any real role for the Communists in government. But the denial did little to convince skeptics, who felt this meeting had more significance than others Berlinguer has had with other Christian Democratic Prime Ministers in the past two years.

The immediate crisis was economic, and the meeting with Berlinguer preceded Moro's meeting with his Cabinet to iron out the austerity measures that were announced later that day. It was clear to observers that to make his austerity program work Moro would need the cooperation of the unions and, thus, the PCI.

As has been the case before, Italy is on the verge of bankruptcy. The country's huge balance of payments deficit and high inflation seemed to have been brought under control at the end of 1975 by stiff deflationary measures, including a since-abolished import deposit scheme. The medicine would seem to have been too stiff, since the country's long-term economic recession increased markedly in January, placing a strain on Italy's currency.

The lira, under severe strain during 1974 and part of 1975, has declined in value by more than 25 percent since mid-January. Moro's austerity measures were designed to counteract its rapid devaluation by cutting back on imports and siphoning the equivalent of about $1.8 billion out of the economy through increased taxes on gas, beef, cars, spirits and restaurant meals.

The feeling prevails in some quarters that Italy's economic problems are the direct result of an inability on the part of the Christian Democrats to put together a government that can deal with basic economic matters. In large part, it is a chicken-and-egg question, but it has been clear to experts since June of 1975 that the Christian Democrats are in more trouble than perhaps ever before.

The elections of June 1975 *thrust* Italy to the left in dramatic fashion. The most impressive gains in those elections were made by the Communist Party, whose share of the vote rose to 33.5 percent from the 27.9 percent scored in the regional elections of 1970. Not only did this represent an increase of 5.6 percent, but it also brought the PCI total to within two percent of the Christian Democratic Party (DC), whose total was 35.2 percent compared with 37.9 percent in 1970. The other party registering a significant advance was the Italian Socialist Party (PSI), which increased its total to 12 percent in contrast to its 10.4 percent in 1970.

Even though those elections were held to renew most of the regional, provincial and municipal councils, they had an overwhelming impact on the entire Italian political scene in that they produced the upset of the Christian Democratic Party chairman, enhanced Communist claims to the sharing of power, and forced the issue of "revitalization" on the ruling Christian Democrats.

Before the Christian Democrats could catch their breath, the Socialists, participants in the historic "apertura a sinistra" (opening to the left) in the early 1960s, pulled the rug from under them. Moro's government was toppled on January 7, 1976, when Socialist Party leader Francesco De Martino withdrew his Party's parliamentary support.

On February 11, Moro formed a minority government, thus averting elections that many experts felt would result in further gains for the Communists. It was Italy's 33rd government since World War II. Moro, who had already been Prime Minister four times, changed only two posts in his cabinet. One of those Moro excluded from the Cabinet was former Defense Minister Luigi Gui, who had been linked by Italian newspapers to a Lockheed Aircraft Corp. "payoff." Gui and another former Defense Minister, Social Democrat Mario Tanassi, came under suspicion when it was reported that Lockheed had paid out kickbacks totaling nearly $2 million in 1970 and 1971 to sell Italy 14 C-130 Hercules transport planes.

Italy, in fact, seemed scandal-ridden as 1976 began, and more than ever the scandals were affecting public attitude toward those in power. In large part the public outrage could be attributed to the fact that a great deal of money was flowing to Italian officials from foreign countries.

The first scandal to wrack Italy in 1976 centered around disclosures that the U.S. Central Intelligence Agency had given $75 million since 1947 to major Italian political parties and several individual candidates. Recipients, according to Turin's newspaper *Stampa Sera*, included former Christian Democratic Prime Minister Giulio Andreotti, current Christian Democratic Industry Minister Carlo Donat-Cattin, former President Giuseppe Saragat of the Social Democratic Party, and Vito Scalia, the centrist labor leader. *Stampa Sera* allegations have not been confirmed. It seems clear, however, that General Vito Miceli, former head of Italian intelligence, received $800,000 in 1972 from the U.S. Ambassador to Italy, Graham Martin.

Still another scandal broke early in March when it was revealed that Genesco, the U.S. shoe company, had offered some $16 million to anyone who would take over its troubled subsidiary in Treviso. GEPI, the state financing company for troubled industries, did take over the San Remo subsidiary, but received only half what Genesco reportedly had offered. Reports circulated that the remainder was siphoned off by individuals who promptly pocketed it. Franco Grassini, director general of GEPI, and Francesco Fabbri, a Christian Democratic politician, are under investigation in the matter. Fabbri recently resigned as Undersecretary of the Treasury.

Most observers feel that the repercussions from these scandals will continue to rock Italy for some time to come, while changing the complexion of some of Italy's political parties. Already, Tanassi has been dismissed as leader of the Social Democrats, a post he held for four years. The Social Democrats took that action at the end of their five-day congress in mid-March, charging Tanassi with moving the party too far to the right and reprimanding him for any role he might have played in the Lockheed scandal.

The crisis in the Social Democratic Party is symptomatic of the turmoil within all of Italy's non-Communist parties. The Social Democrats, who claim only about five percent of the vote, are not quite sure how to approach the future, and neither are the others.

The Christian Democrats are a divided party—even on the question of consulting the Communists. And that issue was in no sharper focus as they began their party congress on March 19—the first they have held in three years—to seek a new strategy for regaining political supremacy. Christian Democratic Party Secretary General Benigno Zaccagnini told the opening day session that some Communist involvement in the creation of a "consensus" was necessary. But he stopped short of favoring the "historic compromise," speaking only of a closer government relationship between his party and the Socialists alone. His narrow reelection to the post of Party Secretary indicates he will have strong opposition from the Right Wing, lead by Arnaldo Forlani, to his goal of a stronger alliance with the Socialists, and a dialogue with the Communists.

Immediately following reports of the Moro-Berlinguer meeting on March 19, a U.S. Embassy spokesman in Rome reiterated the Ford Administration's opposition to Communist participation in Italy's government. Such participation, the spokesman said, would "call for a reassessment" of U.S. economic, military and other relations with its NATO ally. Almost simultaneously, West German Foreign Minister Hans-Dietrich Genscher and Luxembourg Prime Minister Gaston Thorn jointly attacked any Communist participation in West European governments. Genscher, head of West Germany's small Free Democratic Party, called collaboration with the Communists "cooperation against democracy."

The U.S. view of the matter was put in sharper focus during Treasury Secretary William Simon's March visit to Rome. Simon went to the Eternal City to discuss the "Safety Net," also known as the Kissinger-Simon Plan, that could enable Italy to draw credits of up to $1.6 billion. Reporters who questioned him there, though, were more interested in his views on Italy's internal politics.

Simon reiterated the Ford-Kissinger position that a Communist accession to power in Italy would alter the relationship between the United States and that country. While he said that the United States would not abandon Italy "in the hour of trouble," he added that the granting of new credits to Italy was "intimately connected" to the adoption of sound economic policies by Italian authorities. And to that he added that economic evaluations could not be made without paying full attention to political aspects.

If the United States is unhappy about the prospect of the "historic compromise," so, too, is the Soviet Union, which often has expressed its distaste for the avowed plan of the Italian (and the French) Communist Party to seek power through the elective process.

The Soviets softened their opposition somewhat on March 1, when Berlinguer met in Moscow with Communist Party chief Leonid Brezhnev. They announced after their meeting that relations between their two parties should be based on "respect for the independence of each of them." Their statement took some—but not much—of the edge off remarks made by Brezhnev a week earlier, when he told the 25th Communist Party Congress there should be no "compromise on matters of principle." That comment was a clear rebuke to the Italian and the French Communists, who have dropped hallowed Marxist slogans and declared themselves in favor of "pluralist" multi-party democracies.

The Italian Communists also repeatedly have denied any plans for further nationalization of industry, and, as to foreign investment, they seem well aware that multinational companies are needed in Italy for their technology and managerial know-how. For these and other reasons, opinions vary considerably as to whether the admission of the Communist Party into the government, even as a junior partner, would jeopardize private enterprise in Italy and foreign investments. While the psychological effect on business could hardly be anything but unsettling, many observers believe that government policy toward industry would remain much the same.

After all is said and done, it is clear that the question of Communist participation will have to be confronted honestly and openly—even if it is rejected—by the Christian Democrats, other Italian parties, the United States, and the Soviet Union. For it just may be, as Berlinguer said in a speech in Genoa on December 21, 1975, that Italy can surmount the recent crises only by allowing the Communists in the government.

Whatever the immediate outcome, many experts feel the next two years most likely will "make or break" the PCI's three-pronged international strategy. The first objective of this strategy is to obtain American acquiescence to a Communist accession to power. They hope for the largest possible degree of legitimization from Washington. The second is a larger global role for Italian-style Communism, particularly for the Italian version of "autonomy" vis-a-vis the Soviet Communist Party. Thirdly, the Italian Communists want to make a gesture of responsibility toward the weaker Socialist parties of Western Europe, whose cooperation is needed to support the Communist-cultivated image of responsiveness to the democratic "rules of the game."

The PCI approach can best be described as circular. The Party's behavior in the internal realm tends to enhance outside acceptance and that acceptance is promptly put to use at home to promote the Party's image as a serious and reasonable force. By and large, the PCI already has convinced a wide enough international sector of the "inevitability" of its accession to power. But, while this achievement promises to make things easier for the Communists in their external relations after sharing power, it does not solve their short-range problem of entering the government with some assurance that the situation will not degenerate and create an internal backlash.

The Communist strategy also is vulnerable to another course of events: should Communist consolidation in the government prove more difficult and, most importantly, should those problems be protracted, the Italian Communist Party would be subjected to increasing pressures from its grass roots, orthodox base. This would present the Italian Communists with a difficult decision: whether to turn the screw, seize power entirely and govern alone, or prolong the consolidation process in order to neutralize any possible reaction early on in the power-sharing experience—with the risk of provoking a split within the party structure.

To understand the stakes one must appreciate the strengths of the three main political blocs that determine the structural transformation underway in Italy. The Catholic bloc comprises the Christian Democratic Party and a large sector of the Italian electorate that is sensitive to the social and moral guidelines of Catholic inspiration. The leftist bloc includes an array of political elements ranging from small groups of Maoists on the extreme left to the fringe elements of the Christian Democratic Party itself. Its main component is the PCI. The third bloc, a minor entity in political terms but a very vocal one ideologically, is the right, whose main component is the Movimento Sociale Italiano (MSI).

For all practical purposes, the third bloc has ceased to play a political role outside Italy. Its last involvement in international politics occurred with the attempt by U.S. Ambassador Graham Martin to influence the parliamentary elections of 1972 by covertly financing various parties as well as the intelligence chief, Vito Micelli. The fatal predicament of the Italian right was nowhere more evident than in the United States in September 1975 when MSI leader Giorgio Almirante made a private visit to the United States. When Almirante was received at the Executive Office Building by an official of the National Security Council, the resulting outcry in Italy greatly embarrassed the American Embassy.

The Catholic bloc is the natural counterforce to the Communists, but while the Communists have been eager and indeed able to articulate an international role, the Christian Democratic leadership has lost touch with the fast-changing realities of the world. As a result, the Communists have pressed their international strategy, differentiating themselves from the Soviet Communist Party while gaining political solidarity and tactical cooperation in the Western European political arena.

The resistance of the Ford Administration, and especially the consistent opposition of U.S. Secretary of State Henry Kissinger, has prevented the Communists from reaching their paramount objective: that of compelling American leadership to admit that a strong Italy, by virtue of Communist participation in the government combined with Communist guarantees of democratic fair play, is preferable to an Italy plagued by ineffectual governments. The logical corollary of this argument is that a well-governed and economically sound Italy would be worth much more to the United States as a reliable NATO ally. The United States has ignored this not-too-subtle overture, but the Communists have continued to profess their acceptance of NATO, practically without conditions. To be sure, they have not said what kind of NATO they visualize, nor have they tried to reconcile the purpose of NATO as an alliance originally constituted to oppose the expansionist policies of the Soviet Union in Europe. For all practical purposes, the Italian Communists have found a convenient tool in the Cold War to override any and all arguments by anti-Communist forces. At times, they have even taken on the Church.

In November 1975, the Communist Party paper *L'Unita* accused the Vicar of Rome, Ugo Cardinal Poletti, of "intervening" in Italian political life and thereby committing a "constitutional violation," violating the distinction between the "ecclesiastical and state orders." But the same paper also found it politically expedient on occasion to justify the efforts of important sectors of the Christian Democratic Party to give a "lay" orientation to the party. The distinction is attributed to Pope John XXIII and relates to the separation between "ideologies" and "historical movements." In other words, the Italian Communists have claimed the right to establish a working relationship with the "Catholic organized masses," while denying the Vatican any right to "intervene in the political arena." The Communists constantly refer to Pacem in Terris in their recurring attempt to exorcize the warnings of the Roman Catholic Church concerning the incompatibility of Catholicism and Marxism.

The opposition of the Catholic Church, however, has become feeble following its bungling of the divorce referendum, which some quarters felt only accelerated the Christian Democrats' electoral deterioration. At the same time, however, the "liturgical" preoccupation of the Italian Communists concerns Moscow, and the attitude of the Soviet Communist ideologists vis-a-vis the West European Communist parties undoubtedly leaves the Italian Communists fidgeting.

But the fact remains that the PCI has been developing a clever and coherent policy since Enrico Berlinguer took over as Party leader. The strategy he devised is commonly referred to as "this historic compromise," but there is much more behind it than the potential Catholic convergence. It has been based upon a close and detailed analysis of the country's social development.

In the span of a quarter century, from 1949 to 1974, the working class ceased to occupy the priority position in the Communist strategy—a strategy that had carefully nourished its ideological appeal to the Italian working class and constructed a solid political launching platform with the giant Labor Confederation (Conferazione Generale Italiana del Lavoro). The PCI appeal shifted to the middle class: civil servants, small businessmen, artisans, middle level managers, and artists. While the Communist-dominated labor union followed its "egalitarian" Marxist inspiration, filling the gap between blue collar and white collar workers, the PCI pushed its suasive campaign toward independent businessmen and professionals, articulating its dual theme of economic development and social progress. The dialogue could then be carried up to the highest levels of Italian industrial and financial management. Thus, the "reasonableness" of the Italian Communists became the cornerstone for a new strategy phase.

Whenever they were asked what had happened to the ideological starting point of a "dictatorship of the proletariat," they responded that their concept always had been that of the "hegemony of the working class." And by that they meant the "capacity of the working class to solve the national problems, and consequently to attain an hegemonic position in the context of other forces."

This statement was made last fall by Sergio Segre, the "Foreign Minister" of the PCI, in an interview with an Austrian correspondent. Segre also was asked what the PCI would do, assuming it became part of the government, in the event of an unfavorable vote. Segre replied that the Communists could not provide a "notarized pledge" on this question, but could point to a series of "guarantees" resulting from its policies and the history of the PCI. Segre again restated the underlying argument for the Communist insistence on the "historic compromise": "The Italian crisis is so deep that no political force alone can solve it."

Two questions must be asked about a Communist rise to power in the government: one is their willingness to relinquish power under pressure or following a downturn at the polls. The other has to do with the composition of the opposition, which is all important to the Communists. In an interview given to the Rome correspondent of the London Times, at the end of 1975, Berlinguer said, "Most of all, now, Italy needs a government rather than an opposition . . . . A good government never will be able to abolish the opposition but certainly will be able to reduce it." His position is just as flexible in the area of foreign policy. The Communists do not want to raise the problem of Italian withdrawal from NATO because it would be "unrealistic" and because unilateral moves possibly could compromise the balance that allows international détente. "It is better to let the process of détente run its course with the uselessness of military alliances," Berlinguer has emphasized. "We are in favor of European integration, but we look at it as part of a process of democratic transformations within the Community and the member countries."

This remark was clearly aimed at neutralizing a long-held conviction that, once inserted into the European framework, the problem would become more manageable. Therefore, the Communists clearly try to place themselves in position to benefit both from the political adherence to the Western democratic principles of the Community's institutions, and from the increasing economic and social differentiation among the nine member nations.

The attitude of the PCI towards the Soviet Union and the Soviet Communist Party deserves attention from two different angles, the internal or italian, and the international. On the first score, Berlinguer keeps repeating that the PCI does not look at the Soviet Communist Party as the "guiding party." But then he quickly adds, "No Communist Party, including the Soviet Party, is in a position of influential leadership." In the international realm, however, the leadership of the Italian Communist Party can hardly be discounted in terms of a coordinated strategy of the West European Communist parties. Berlinguer's strategy, it must be stressed, is to counteract the claim of the anti-Communist forces, and of Kissinger in particular, that the "democratic" evolution of the PCI is "all tactics." The joint statement signed in November by Berlinguer and the Secretary General of the French Communist Party, Georges Marchais, is a long-term definition of common political objectives that look well beyond the controversial meeting of the European Communist parties.

The statement was nothing new for the PCI, while it represents a radical turn-about in the French position. The document proclaims the allegiance of the two parties to "the liberty of thought and expression, of the press, of meeting and association, the right to demonstrate, the free movement of persons inside and outside their country, the inviolability of private life, of religious liberties, the total freedom of expression of currents of thought and of every philosophical, cultural and artistic opinion."

The French renunciation of the old-time formula of the "dictatorship of the proletariat" put the French Communists squarely in Berlinguer's camp and quickly provoked a Soviet mission to Rome. Vadim Zagladin, deputy chief of the section for international relations of the Soviet Communist Party, showed up in the Italian capital with two other Soviet Party functionaires. Ostensibly, they were in Rome for a testimonial event, but on December 12 Zagladin was closeted in a long meeting with Berlinguer, Giancarlo Pajetta and Segre. L'Unita said the meeting was conducive to "an exchange of views on the international situation and the problems of the workers' movement." But more could be found in an article that Zagladin wrote under a pen name, in the weekly Novoe Vremja. It stated that "although the Communist parties operate in different conditions and adopt different strategic decisions, nonetheless they remain Communist parties." He added: "Although they realize the widest alliances and coalitions, they remain faithful to the Marxist-Leninist ideology and to their revolutionary principles." This enunciation of fundamental Marxist-Leninist doctrine was in open contradiction to the Berlinguer-Marchais declaration, which stated: "The French and Italian Communists favor the plurality of political parties, the right of the opposition parties to exist and to act, the free formation of majorities and minorities and the possibility of their alternating democratically, the lay character and democratic functioning of the state and the independence of justice."

The matrix for the convergence of the Italian and French Communist Parties can be found in the original enunciation of the "historic compromise" by Berlinguer in the fall of 1973, shortly after the overthrow of Salvador Allende's Marxist government in Chile. Berlinguer called for "collaboration and agreement" among the popular forces of Communist and Socialist inspiration and the popular forces of Catholic inspiration "together with the formations of other Democratic organizations."

The PCI clearly has become a "mass party" on the basis of the principles that underlie the "historic compromise," i.e. "collaboration and agreement" with the popular Catholic forces. But first and foremost in the minds of the Communist leaders is their preoccupation with preserving their credibility with the Party base and the electorate at large. For this reason, the PCI does not want to get involved with the open leadership of the labor unions, but, rather, describes the duty of the Party as that of convincing the workers themselves to take responsibility for the process of economic conversion in the interest of the country. In fact, all Italian Communist leaders have seized the high ground in the latest economic downturn, warning that the fall of the Moro government, and the subsequent long political crisis, would open the door to a period of dangerous political confusion in a phase of economic prostration.

The Italian Communists have a clear idea of Italy's need for continued growth and rising real incomes, and Italy depends totally on the Western economic system to achieve its growth. Given the depressed state of the Italian economy, it is imperative to keep the current account deficits to manageable levels by means of credits from the International Monetary Fund and other private financial markets of the West. The economic problem poses a difficult cause-and-effect relationship for the Italian Communists. On the one hand, the failure of the governing coalitions to assure a steady rise in the standard of living and to implement effective reforms gives a push to the political slide to the left. On the other hand, this trend worsens the economic situation as it cuts down capital investment drastically and increases capital flight. In turn, this causes unemployment and aggravates the balance of payments deficit.

It is generally agreed that a Communist-dominated government in Italy could not do without the economic factors that maintain the free market economy. Still, the Italian Communists are making good political capital out of their proposed new model for economic development, which would accomplish a restructuring of the Italian economy without altering the basic factors of production. But they have yet to reconcile the relationship between the present Communist posture, which does not deny a large measure of "democratic centralism," and pressures from the grass roots and the local Communist administrations for wide-ranging Socialist reform. The choice is further complicated by the inherent contradiction in the Soviet Socialist model, which still holds validity for a large part of the Italian Communist membership.

The stresses and strains within the Italian Communist Party have become visible, in fact, through the juxtaposition of the increasing power of Communist-dominated regional and municipal administrations and the central power structure. These seeds of division may begin to sprout as the hard choices confront the Party.

So far, the decision of the Christian Democrats to keep the Communists from sharing power, although trying to give them some responsibilities, has allowed Berlinguer to escape a real clarification of what the Communists would do if they were to share it, and to what levels the PCI would push the socialization of production and distribution.

The basic question, it would seem, is whether Soviet Communism wants to see the Italian Communists try their hand in a free society. The Soviet Union's behavior has fueled the ideological controversies in the Communist field. This has allowed the Western Communists, and the Italian Communists in particular, to eschew any action or position that would attest to the existence of a strong link with the Soviet Communist Party, thereby increasing their chances of electoral success. Brezhnev long has pressed for a document that would testify to the unity of strategy and tactics among all Communist Parties—obviously inspired by the Soviet "Socialist model." But to the extent that ideological debate does not impair the fundamental directive of Eastern European Communist states, i.e. of consolidating their control over all possible liberalizing temptations, the Soviet Union supports the national tactics of the Western European countries and their unorthodox combinations.

For all the incompatibility of the orthodox revolutionary activism and the identification of Italian and French Communists with other progressive forces of the Left, the Soviet Union has yet to condemn the "foreign policy" of the Italian Communist Party and its not very subtle search for legitimization by the United States.

What the PCI has done is to shift its international strategy from the European institutions, which are languishing somewhat, to a much larger realm involving U.S. interests. The Communists do not want simply to end the "intransigence" of American policy towards a governmental role for the PCI, but, rather, want an entirely new policy that would make it easier for them to follow a line of "autonomy" from the Soviet Union and to enjoy material support from the capitalist West.

47

The Communist weekly *Rinascita* stated last November that the United States simply is trying to prevent the formation and consolidation of a "new bloc of political and social forces," which could open the way to a social, economic and political "renovation" in the European continent. More cautious observers feel that the long-term implication of this thesis is clear enough: the "new bloc" would guarantee the strengthening of the Italian Communist "autonomy," while promoting the long-run interest of the Soviet Union to modify the balance of power in Europe and to weaken, and eventually sever, the Atlantic ties. At a minimum, Soviet interests and PCI strategy certainly do not clash. In time, the possible symbiosis may manifest itself.

The real question facing the United States is not how to stem the Communist push to power in Italy (certainly not with covert financial intervention), but, rather, how to prevent the Italian Communists from building a "new bloc of political and social forces" in open contrast to the economic and military arrangements and cooperation among the Western democracies. A clear and vigorous statement to this effect would be far more effective than a mere containing action in Italy, for the problems are rapidly becoming larger than that of Washington's ability simply to control Communist participation in the Rome government.

Appendix

Opening Remarks:
Dr. Ray S. Cline

I want to welcome you all on behalf of the Georgetown University Center for Strategic and International Studies. This Center is a nonprofit, educational institution dedicated to enhancing public understanding of strategic and international affairs by promoting objective nonpartisan research and seminar discussions on public policy issues confronting the United States. Our approach is interdisciplinary in that we examine the economic, military, and political aspects of international issues as one interrelated whole. This Center takes no policy positions but encourages presentation of every reasonable viewpoint.

A few months ago this Center published the first book which I have written since resigning from the State Department in 1973, an analysis of international relationships called *World Power Assessment*. In it I stressed that the international influence of countries depends not only on their territorial, demographic, economic, and military resources, but even more on the clarity with which nations see strategic issues and are successful in political mobilization of national will to meet strategic challenges.

Today we are examining trends affecting the political stability of one of the great Western industrial democracies, Italy. This important nation is tied to the United States and American international interests by the very large Italian ethnic component in our population, the contribution to our way of life from these Italian-Americans as well as from the common cultural heritage of Roman civilization, a similar political system of representative government within a free and open society, extensive commercial and investment links between the two countries, and a solemn, twenty-seven-year-old mutual defense treaty.

Surely it is our responsibility in the United States to ponder thoughtfully the strategic issues at stake in present-day Italian political trends of an unprecedented character. We must see our strategic interests clearly if we are to exercise our great power wisely. We must also pay closest attention to the probable effect of current Italian developments on the cohesion of national political will throughout Europe and the Mediterranean. In the international concerns of this close ally, just as in our own, political will is a vital factor and the most elusive factor in regional security and economic welfare. The political stability of any major nation is a legitimate agenda item in international affairs.

In the ongoing program here at Georgetown whereby we study vital issues of public policy in every aspect of strategic and international affairs, I can think of no theme that has emerged in recent months with greater clarity and urgency than this one: what are the prospects for political stability in Italy, and what does this mean for the European and Mediterranean world in which the United States has crucial strategic interests at stake?

Appendix

Opening Remarks:
The Hon. John B. Connally

In this first symposium on Vital Issues we focus on international concerns which will greatly influence the course of American foreign policy over the remainder of this decade. While they are centered in one region, from the Levant to the Iberian Peninsula, these concerns affect all regions of the world. They are at once political, military, economic and social. In a very real way they are also religious, and I speak not only of Lebanon and its tragic civil war but of the Vatican itself. They are, of course, intensely ideological, because they represent a battleground for the moral and spiritual allegiance of millions of people. They involve three continents directly and a fourth continent less directly but no less importantly. And the region with which we deal in these discussions was the cradle of civilization. It is not beyond reason that it could also become its grave.

It is an honor for me to share this platform with such distinguished experts on the Mediterranean. My role is that of moderator, but in these preliminary remarks I will sketch the outline of our discussion and express some personal views which led me to recommend that the organization I created, called Vital Issues, begin its series of symposia around the nation by joining Georgetown University in this analysis of Mediterrranean security.

It is my belief that we have entered an extremely dangerous period of history—comparable, in fact, to the decade prior to the Second World War. It disturbs me, frankly, that many Americans are unwilling to accept the warning signs. Perhaps we are so preoccupied with our domestic troubles that we cannot properly relate these problems to the whole issue of security and peace. Perhaps we are so anxious to reject the Cold War mentality of a few years ago that we are blind to the expansionist policies of the Soviet Union.

Whatever the reasons for our malaise, consider the parallels of the 1970s and the 1930s—

—A slow economy not only in America, but throughout the industrialized world;

—The dramatic decline of the United Nations as a credible peacekeeping agency;

—Political unrest in many volatile areas of the globe;

—Aggressive military and political moves by a major totalitarian power on a crusade which is both imperialistic and idealogical;

—The re-emergence of isolationism in America, coupled with a relentless attack on the defense establishment.

It seems apparent to me, my friends, that we have indeed moved quietly and almost unnoticed into a new and perilous era—conceivably, in fact, an era of reckoning for Western civilization—and freedom.

The expansionism of our adversaries should be as obvious as the aggressive new order of Germany and Japan four decades ago. I credit the Soviets with remarkable military and political progress. They have smothered democratic influence in the United Nations. They have straddled our vital supply lines on both sides of the African continent under the guise of supporting movements for national liberation. They have persuaded their client state, Cuba, to furnish a surrogate army for its aggressive designs. They have intensified political activity among our NATO allies, and while they have been turned back for the time being in Portugal, there will be no respite anywhere on the southern flank of the Alliance. All in all, this has been a rewarding decade for Soviet expansionism, notwithstanding the conflict with China and the pullback in Egypt.

I do not know a single American who does not want an end to the arms race. I do not know a single American who wishes détente to fail, and who does not prefer to talk of commerce rather than confrontation. But I am concerned that we are too quick to draw back from the dangers that threaten us over the rim of the world. I am concerned that we doubt our capacity to lead—that we have wearied of the burden, just as the British grew weary, and that we are willing to settle for less responsibility at the very time our adversaries want more.

We cannot let this happen. We must begin to approach foreign policy with as much unity as free speech and free assembly permit. We must be militarily strong because the Soviet Union has never subscribed to the notion that the meek will inherit the earth. We must put our economic house in order and help restore the vitality of our friends and allies. We must generate new ideas and new policies on world trade, predicated on national self-interest and fair treatment for all of the partners in the enterprise.

This is a political challenge and a moral challenge. I submit to you that our awareness of its serious implications—our willingness to renew our responsibilities of economic and military leadership in a divided world—may well determine whether truly there will be peace in our time or the terrible alternative.

Nowhere is our responsibility and our national interest more clear than in Western Europe and along the southern edge of NATO. In examining this region we will move through one area after another of conflict and political unrest. It is as if all of the problems of the world suddenly have descended on the countries of the Mediterranean.

Lebanon: Religious and political warfare which has nearly destroyed a prosperous and enlightened nation.

Israel and its neighbors: Continuing tension despite the agreement in the Sinai and now amplified by the probability of nuclear weapons in the Middle East.

Cyprus: Recovering from war but the central object of division between two NATO allies, Greece and Turkey.

Yugoslavia: Clinging doggedly to its hard-won independence within the Communist bloc, but what happens after Tito is gone?

North Africa: Beset by jealousies and political differences among Arab nations with the growing danger of war between Algeria and Morocco over the former Spanish Sahara.

Spain: Struggling awkwardly toward greater freedom following the death of Franco, but plagued by political turmoil and ripe for internal conflicts greater than at any time since the civil war ended in 1939.

Portugal: Badly shaken by a near Communist takeover, now striving to maintain a chance for democratic stability in the face of severe economic problems.

France: Saved at its last election by only a single percentage point from a leftist government with strong ties to the Communist Party.

Italy: Millions of urban residents already governed by Communists, moving toward crucial elections which may well bring Communists into national power with dire consequences for the Western Alliance.

The Vatican: Looking toward the possibility of co-existence with a secular government whose Russian founders and patrons rose to power as persecutors of all religious belief.

So all of these circumstances, some of which have reached the crisis level, pose many questions for the American people.

If Italy is to admit Communists to positions of power in the government, what of our military bases there? Will the Christian Democrats of Italy become nothing more than the Mensheviks of 1917 Russia, or the Social Democrats of 1948 Czechoslovakia?

53

How long will the "benevolent" and "efficient" Communist Party of Italy be concerned with freedom of speech, freedom of the press, and tolerance of other political parties? No other Communist regime in history has demonstrated such liberal tendencies for very long—only long enough to suit its purposes.

To what extent should the people of the United States react to the political crisis in Italy? Is it any of our business?

Have we lost naval dominance in the Mediterranean to the growing fleet of Russian warships—including their first aircraft carrier? What is the effect on the balance of power on the eastern end of the Mediterranean? Is Israel then in an untenable position?

What happens in France if Mitterrand and Marchais put together a left-wing coalition to rule a highly centralized nation which could easily become a police state?

It is conceivable that many of these flash points in Southern Europe, the Middle East and Africa will become less dangerous in time. It is conceivable that the balance of power will remain more or less constant in spite of temporary setbacks to the free world.

We should not overreact to any given situation. We should not assume that the American response to every undesirable occurrence around the world should be identical in all respects. We should not assume automatically that the United States can—or should try to—prevent every move by the Soviet Union to carry out a foreign policy the Soviet Union believes to be in its national interest. We should not be obliged, as a matter of course, to match every Russian submarine with an American submarine, every Russian division in the Warsaw Pact nations with an American division in Western Europe.

But it is our responsibility to consider seriously every evidence of Soviet expansionism—to weigh its effect upon us and our allies, to analyze its consequences, to study the options in foreign policy and military policy which protect our own interests and the interests of our friends.

Had England and France done this in 1936 and 1938 perhaps there would never have been a Second World War. Had the United States not been so preoccupied with its internal woes, and so afflicted with blind isolationism, perhaps the Axis powers would have been more wary of starting such a war.

The parallels of the 70s and 30s are not exact, but they are close enough to concern me.

Someday, somehow, the United States must stop misleading its adversaries by inconsistent and uncertain words and deeds. It must make itself plain. It must stop permitting rank partisanship to interfere with extremely serious foreign policy. It must show maturity in world affairs. It must be alert, vital, open-handed and even-handed—and loyal to the cause it espouses, in times of darkness as well as sunshine.

I hope that this symposium is conducted in that spirit. I believe that forums such as this can contribute to a greater understanding of the challenges of American diplomacy at a time when clarity is essential and consistency is the mother of success.

Appendix

U.S. Foreign Policy and Italy: An Address by the Honorable Clare Boothe Luce

Those of you who attended the panel discussion this afternoon were briefed on the problems confronting Italy today and tomorrow by four of what might be called the best brains in the business. If I had known, when I accepted Dr. Cline's invitation to give the wind-up talk, that I would be following Mr. Colby, Admiral Rivero, Ms. Claire Sterling, and Governor Connally, I would have refused—on the grounds that any speaker whose name wasn't Henry would be anti-climactic.

Happily for me, Dr. Cline assured me a few days ago that I need not confine myself specifically to the Italian problem, but was free to put before the conferees any thoughts broadly relevant to the subject.

So, with your indulgence I will venture a few personal opinions about U.S. foreign policy. For, in the final analysis, it is in the context of U.S. foreign policy today that the Italian people will make their decision whether or not to opt for the "historic compromise" with Communism.

Now a great humorist of my youth, Robert Benchley, once wrote a book spoofing the work of a jungle explorer which, in that long-ago time, was a big best seller. Benchley's book was called, "Up and Down the Alimentary Canal with Benchley." Among the many fantastic animals Benchley described on his voyage was a remarkable creature he called the Killyloo bird. This very clever bird had the habit of flying backwards at the start of every new flight. This, Benchley explained, was because until it had seen where it had been, it couldn't be sure of where it was going.

Let us, like the Killyloo bird, take a short backward flight over the field of U.S. foreign policy, in order to see where we—and Italy—are going.

The United States' East-West policy which Détente officially superseded was Containment. This policy, as it evolved under the leadership of four presidents, lasted 25 years. It was America's global response to the global threat of world revolutionary Communism. Unlike Détente—the word that just won't go

57

away—the word Containment was a wonderfully *un*ambiguous word. It was a word, which, applied to U.S. policy, was not only descriptive but also prescriptive. Every American, and every foreigner, knew not only what Containment meant, but who and what were to be contained. There was no confusion anywhere about the policy's objective. It was to prevent the ideological and military expansion of totalitarianism into the non-Communist or "free world," by peaceful or cold war methods if possible, by hot war if Communist aggression made it necessary.

At home and abroad everyone understood on what the success of the policy depended.

First, it depended on the maintenance of U.S. military superiority in the air, on the sea, and in nuclear weaponry, and on the contribution of land power and air and naval bases by our allies in Europe and Asia. *Secondly,* the containment of Communist ideological, or political, expansion depended on U.S. economic aid to the war stricken nations and the impoverished countries outside the Iron Curtain, who might otherwise, in desperation, opt for totalitarian solutions. *Thirdly,* and most importantly, its success depended on the *will* of the American people and their leaders to pursue the policy with zeal and fidelity, and to make such sacrifices of blood or treasure as circumstances might require.

Containment was both an idealistic and a realistic policy. It was designed to meet the Communist global challenge at every level—military, political, and ideological.

Walter Lippmann once described U.S. foreign policy as the Shield of the Republic. For more than 20 years the policy of Containment held the Shield of the Republic not only over our own lives and liberties, but over the lives and liberties of more than a billion other people. It encouraged scores of new nations, rising from the ruins of the old colonial system, to establish governments and institutions congruent with democratic ideals, and aided them to begin developing their own resources. It economically rehabilitated our three great world war enemies—Japan, Germany and Italy—and brought them into the democratic fold. Thanks to Containment and its creation of NATO, there has been no war in Europe for 30 years—the longest period of peace Europe has known in its entire history.

Despite the multi-billion dollar cost of Containment, the 50s and 60s became the most prosperous years most of the Western nations, and many other free world countries, had ever known. In 1947, the first year of Containment, the American GNP was 468.3 billion dollars; in 1972, the eighth year of our involvement in Vietnam, our GNP was 1 trillion, 171 billion dollars. And in those years, the economic progress of Italy, once known as "the sick man of

Europe," was so great that it was called "the miracle of Europe." Between 1947 and 1972, the year that Containment was officially buried, the Italian Communist Party gained only 8 percent of the vote, and it was enabled to make even this small progress only by renouncing revolutionary methods and pledging itself to uphold freedom of press and speech—and free elections. Containment educated Europe's largest Communist party in the ways of Democracy. And so it was.

History will certainly NOT view Containment as an unsound policy. It did not fail us. We failed it.

The long, ill-conceived, badly fought war in Vietnam eroded the consensus for Containment, and this created a dangerous vacuum in U.S. foreign policy. The Nixon Administration saw that unless a policy could be devised that would offer the American people some hope of ending the East-West struggle without seeming to abandon our role of world leadership, the force of public opinion would create de facto a U.S. policy of Isolationism. Some policy had to be devised consistent with political realities at home and abroad. Something, so to speak, East of Containment, yet West of Isolationism. In 1972, the policy vacuum was filled by Détente. It might be more accurate to say that it was filled by Dr. Kissinger and his "shuttle diplomacy."

From its inception, no U.S. foreign policy has ever been harder to come to grips with, or caused so much semantic confusion. Asked in 1973 by a Senate Committee to explain his own interpretation of Détente, Dr. Kissinger replied, "Détente is a process, not a final condition." But I think you will agree that the claim made for this process was that—for the price of a concession here and a concession there, it would progressively produce a mutual "relaxation" of political and military tensions with the USSR which would lead to a "generation of peace."

The process of Détente is now in its fourth year. The Soviets and the Cubans are in Angola. The Syrians have moved into Lebanon. The PLO has become a Soviet client. And once again, as the war clouds gather over the Middle East, Israel faces a grave hour of peril. The Soviets, who have steadily continued to enlarge their land, air and naval war machine, have started a buildup of military strength in Eastern Europe. The Chinese have entertained Mr. Nixon in order to get across to the White House that Soviet Russia is still very much in the world-domination business. The North Koreans are itching to go. India has passed into the Soviet orbit and is no longer in the democratic fold. The dominoes are still falling in Southeast Asia. In Europe, Portugal, a NATO member, is not yet safely off the democratic danger list. Cyprus and Turkey have not yet composed their differences, and we are threatened with the loss of our Turkish military and intelligence-collection bases. NATO is in a state of shocking disarray. The GNP growth rate in every Western country has fallen, and all are plagued by inflation and unemployment.

And—the subject of the day—Italy: During Détente the Communist Party in Italy gained an astounding 6 percent more of the vote, and is on the verge of the "historic compromise."

Finally, the failure of the process of Détente has become so visible that President Ford has ordered the State Department to drop the *word* from our diplomatic vocabulary, and to use the term "Peace Through Strength" instead. The truth of the matter is that once again, there is a vacuum in U.S. foreign policy which, if it is not soon filled by a policy addressed to the international realities, will lead on the Soviet Installment Plan, to the isolation of America.

There would be no Italian Communist problem if there were no Soviet Union—determined to achieve hegemony over the Middle East and the oil that is the lifeblood of Europe's economy; determined to make the Mediterranean a Russian lake; determined to collapse NATO; determined as yesterday, today, and tomorrow—in Brezhnev's own words—to bring about "the triumph of world socialism" under Soviet leadership.

There would be no Italian Communist problem if the Italian people did not feel that the United States has no policy today that promises them any hope that they will not, in the end, be relentlessly drawn into the orbit of Moscow.

In private conversations with European statesmen, Dr. Kissinger is reported to have propounded a new domino theory: He is said to feel that the entrance of the Communists into the Italian government could have a political domino effect in France and West Germany which would lead to the withdrawal of American forces from those two countries and make the continuance of the 25-year-old Western Alliance, created by Containment, impossible. It was, therefore, American policy, he said, to oppose "the historic compromise with Communism" in Italy as long as possible. When it was pointed out to him that the United States *itself* had reached an "historic compromise" with the Soviets at Helsinki, he is reputed to have replied that we cannot avoid dealing with Communists *after* they come to power.

Considering that our dealings with the Soviets have been wonderfully generous, and have included vast shipments of wheat below world prices, a one-way extension of valuable technology, and the granting of massive credits, it is not surprising that many Italians feel that Italy might derive more economic and political consideration from the United States if Italy *did* become a Communist power.

There is no shadow of doubt that Italy's best hope of a stable and reasonably prosperous economy and of maintaining its democratic liberties depends on its remaining within the framework of a strong, independent, and democratic Europe. Again, thanks to the success of Containment, which helped create the European Economic Community as well as NATO, even the Italian Communists seem to believe this—or at any rate, say they do.

On the other hand, there is no question where they would stand if push came to shove, and the Soviets achieved domination of the Mediterranean.

Also, to repeat, there is no question that this is precisely what the USSR intends to do. In fact, there is now only one open question in Italy, in Europe, in Africa, in Asia—and in Latin America: Do the American people, or do they *not*, have the will to resist Soviet imperialism?

I believe that we will discover the answer to that momentous question by the time the next President is elected. It will be revealed to us in the foreign policy stand taken by the winning candidate. For no candidate is going to win unless his foreign policy views reflect the will of the people.

I am today more optimistic than I was a year ago that the American people are recovering from the trauma of Vietnam and are once again preparing themselves to shoulder the task of world leadership. We are the richest, the strongest, the freest nation in the world. If it is not our destiny to be the guardian of freedom in what is left of the free world, whose destiny is it?

I have a hunch—it is nothing more—that the Italian people, who also love their freedom well, are going to have the wisdom to postpone the "historic compromise" until the answer to this great question is given in November, by the American people.

List of Participants

Peter Abbruzzese
Office of Congressman Wayne Hays

Hon. Theodore Achilles
Atlantic Council of the
United States

**Hon. Bill Alexander and
Mrs. Alexander**
U.S. Congress

John Backer
Office of Senator Bill Brock

Michael Balzano
ACTION

William Baroody
American Enterprise Institute

R. Admiral John Barrow
Department of the Navy

Charles Bartlett
Chicago Daily News

Robert Bartley
Wall Street Journal

**Hon. Henry Bellmon and
Mrs. Bellmon**
U.S. Senate

Frank Blunt
International Ltd.

Avis Bohlen
U.S. Arms Control and
Disarmament Agency

T. Edward Braswell
Senate Armed Services Committee

Jerome Breiter
Hercules, Inc.

Elizabeth Brownstein
Evening Edition, WETA

Admiral Arleigh Burke, USN (Ret.)
CSIS Chairman Emeritus

Mr. & Mrs. Horace Busby
Busby Associates

Brewster Campbell
Bank of America

Nicholas Campbell
EXXON Corporation

James Cary
Copley News Service

Mr. & Mrs. William Casey
President's Foreign
Intelligence Advisory Board;
Counsel to the Law Firm of
Rogers and Wells

Anna Chennault
Flying Tiger Line, Inc.

Lt. Col. Patrick Chisolm
National War College

Judy Cline
Central Intelligence Agency

Marjorie Cline
National Geographic Magazine

Sibyl Cline
Drug Abuse Council

Robert Cohoes
U.S. Information Agency

Mrs. William Colby

Jim Connally

Mrs. John Connally

Mr. & Mrs. Robert Coonrod
U.S. Information Agency

David Corcoran
Sterling Drug International

Hon. Thomas Corcoran
Corcoran, Youngman & Rowe

Fred Crawford
Emory University

Ken Crosby
Merrill, Lynch, Pierce,
Fenner and Smith

Hon. Tom Curtis & Mrs. Curtis
Federal Election Commission

Nick Daniloff
United Press International

Thomas Dine
Senate Budget Committee

James Donley
Donley Communications Corp.

Hon. Eleanor Lansing Dulles
Retired Diplomat

Captain James Elfelt
Department of the Navy

Commander Howard Eldredge
Department of the Navy

Edmund Fawcett
The Economist

Hon. Henry Fowler
Former Secretary of the Treasury

Philip Foisie
The Washington Post

Lawrence Fox
National Association of
Manufacturers

Paul Freedenberg
Office of Senator J. Bennett
Johnston

Jack Gardner
International Telephone &
Telegraph

Michael Gardner
Federal Energy Administration

George Gedda
Associated Press

Jim George
Office of Senator Bill Brock

Bill Gill
Vital Issues of America, Inc.

Whitney Goit
Department of State

General Daniel Graham
University of Miami Center for
Advanced International Studies

Katharine Graham
Chairman of the Board
The Washington Post

Albert Grasseli
Rockwell International

Charles Gunning
Canadian Broadcasting Company

Stef Halper
Office of Management and Budget

Howard Handleman
U.S. News and World Report

Dale Herspring
Department of State

Hon. Daniel Hofgren
Goldman, Sachs & Company

James Huff
Department of State

George Ingram
House International Relations
Committee

A. W. Jessup
EXXON Corporation

David Jones
Department of State

Wynfred Joshua
Defense Intelligence Agency

Joseph Kingsbury-Smith
Hearst Newspapers

Joseph Keenan
AFL-CIO

Ernest Lefever
The Brookings Institution

Mr. & Mrs. John Lehman
U.S. Arms Control and
Disarmament Agency

James Lenehan
Collins Radio Group,
Rockwell International

Bernard Lewis
Princeton University and
Institute of Advanced Studies

Barry Locke
Smith and Locke Consultants

Edwin Manton
American International Group

Roberto Memmo

Antonio Marinelli
Intercountry Construction
Corporation

Mr. & Mrs. Kenneth Maruyama

Marshall Mays
OPIC

Hon. Robert McClintock
Former U.S. Ambassador to
Venezuela

Hon. James McClure and Mrs. McClure
U.S. Senate

Robert McLaughlin
U.S. Information Agency

Harlan Moen
Department of State

Admiral Thomas Moorer, USN (Ret.)
Former Chairman, Joint Chiefs
of Staff

Gene Mosier
PPG Industries, Inc.

Robert Moss
The Economist

Hon. Robert Murphy
Corning International Corporation

Paul Neuland
Office of the Army Chief of Staff

Joseph Neyhart
W.R. Grace & Company

Frank O'Neil
PPG Industries, Inc.

Robert Osgood
Johns Hopkins University School
for Advanced International Studies

R. Admiral Richard Paddock
Department of the Navy

Major Stuart Perkins
Office of the Secretary of
Defense

Louise Peterson
Defense Intelligence Agency

Vladimir Petrov
George Washington University
Sino-Soviet Institute

John Pond
Department of the Navy

Carol Preece
Federal City College

Robert Rieman
Defense Intelligence Agency

Dr. & Mrs. Hampton Robinson
Texas State Commissioner of
Health

Lawrence Rogers II
Taft Broadcasting Company

Donald Roper
RCA Corporation

Alison Rosenberg
Office of Senator Charles Percy

William Safire
New York Times

Mr. & Mrs. Nathaniel Samuels
Louis Dreyfus Corporation

Mr. & Mrs. Russell Schoch
American Press Institute

William A. Searle
U.S. Arms Control and
Disarmament Agency

William Seebeck
W.R. Grace and Company

John Shea
Department of State

Gaston Sigur
George Washington University
Sino-Soviet Institute

Denney-Wells Spencer
Emory University

Hon. Robert Strauss
Democratic National Committee

Scott Sullivan
Newsweek

Strobe Talbott
Time

David Taylor, Jr.
Mobil Oil Corporation

John Thomas
PPG Industries, Inc.

Michele Thoren
Office of Congressman John Rhodes

Mr. & Mrs. Frank Tonini
U.S. Information Agency

Joan Urban
Catholic University

Jack Valenti
Motion Picture Association
of America

James Wade, Jr.
Department of Defense

Jenonne Walker
Department of State

Don Wallace
Georgetown University Law Center

Stanislaw Wasowski
Georgetown University

Sofia Wasowski
Georgetown University

Hon. Barbara Watson
Former Administrator,
Department of State

Nathan Weissman
Gillette, Inc.

Garland West
Cargill, Inc.

Alan White
Standard Oil of Indiana

Jane Whitmore
Newsweek

F. Lisle Widman
Department of the Treasury

Theodore Wilkinson
Office of the Secretary of
Defense

Mr. & Mrs. Edward Bennett Williams
Williams, Connolly & Califano

Reverend Francis X. Winters, S.J.
Georgetown University

Hon. Marshall Wright
Eaton Corporation

Paul Wolfowitz
U.S. Arms Control and
Disarmament Agency

Felicia Zimmerman
Office of Senator Edward Brooke